Lazarus

Photographs by
Jason Baldinger

OAC Books
Belle, MO
www.osageac.org

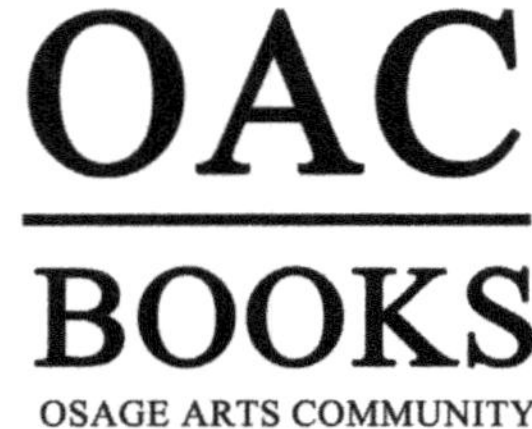

Design, Edits and Layout: Paulette Poullet
With Thanks to: Osage Arts Community, Jason Ryberg,
Paulette Poullet and Rebecca Schumeda

The raising of Lazarus from the dead reminds us that when Jesus is seemingly doing nothing, he is actually doing more than we can fathom. Lazarus is a fitting title for this collection of photos because at first glance you may not notice the subtleties but when you look closer you see multidimensional and thought-provoking images. As you turn the pages, you will encounter an American flag reflected over the word "Prescription," the reminder that "COAL KEEPS THE LIGHTS ON!!!" juxtaposed over a deserted industrial area, a skeleton donning a Santa hat in a display window mirroring a ghost town and many more awe-striking photographs. Baldinger's pieces give pause as they explore the American experience, predominately in the rust belt, a region that encountered severe industrial decline for decades. They show how a once bustling landscape has been reduced to a ghost town.

Ironically it is what is missing from the photos that stand out the most. Outside storefront windows, along sidewalks, beside houses, apartments, and factories, you will not see human beings. There are mannequins and statues which almost act as bookmarks in the story and emphasize human abandonment. The signs on storefront windows also seem to reveal part of the narrative: Auction: Sunday, October 21st, faith, temporarily closed, custom picture framing, Lazarus, THIS PLACE MATTERS, STOP LOOK SAVE, HOMEMADE PIE AND CAKE, COLD BEER TO GO, and Last Days Ministries. While you look through these pictures, you can't help but be reminded of the Fred R. Barnard's saying "One Look is Worth a Thousand Words," because you will spend time appreciating each piece and taking it all the offerings.

Each photo is itself a poem that documents the landscape of deteriorating Americana. Baldinger's decision to capture these images using a reflective technique not only adds dimension but also adds an interesting spin on the subject matter. These pieces seem to invite the reader to reconsider their perspective on the disappearance of working-class society in this country. Baldinger asks us to consider what is missing in our country that is allowing for the widening gap between rich and poor, allowing so many to fall through the cracks, to disappear.

Baldinger's photos take the viewer outside of themselves in the same way his poetry invites the reader to step outside of their narrow view and into the world around them. What I like best about these photos is how they highlight details that could easily go unnoticed if you were lackadaisically walking the same landscape as Baldinger. His scrupulous eye zones in on the minutiae that helps the observer to reevaluate their first impressions of society. His poetry most notably celebrates and reacquaints readers with the steel city, the working class, jazz music, iconic figures on the fringes, and travel, specifically in the rust belt and he carries out the same undertaking in his photos. While I am not equating Baldinger to Jesus, he does in a strange way raise American working-class society's overlooked struggles to the forefront in these photos allowing us the onlooker to consider the repercussions of this loss.

Rebecca Schumejda
Author of *Sentenced*

Let's disappear past the shadows
Where only the damage stays

The Delines
Past the Shadows

Lazarus wasn't grateful for his second wind

American Music Club
I've Been A Mess

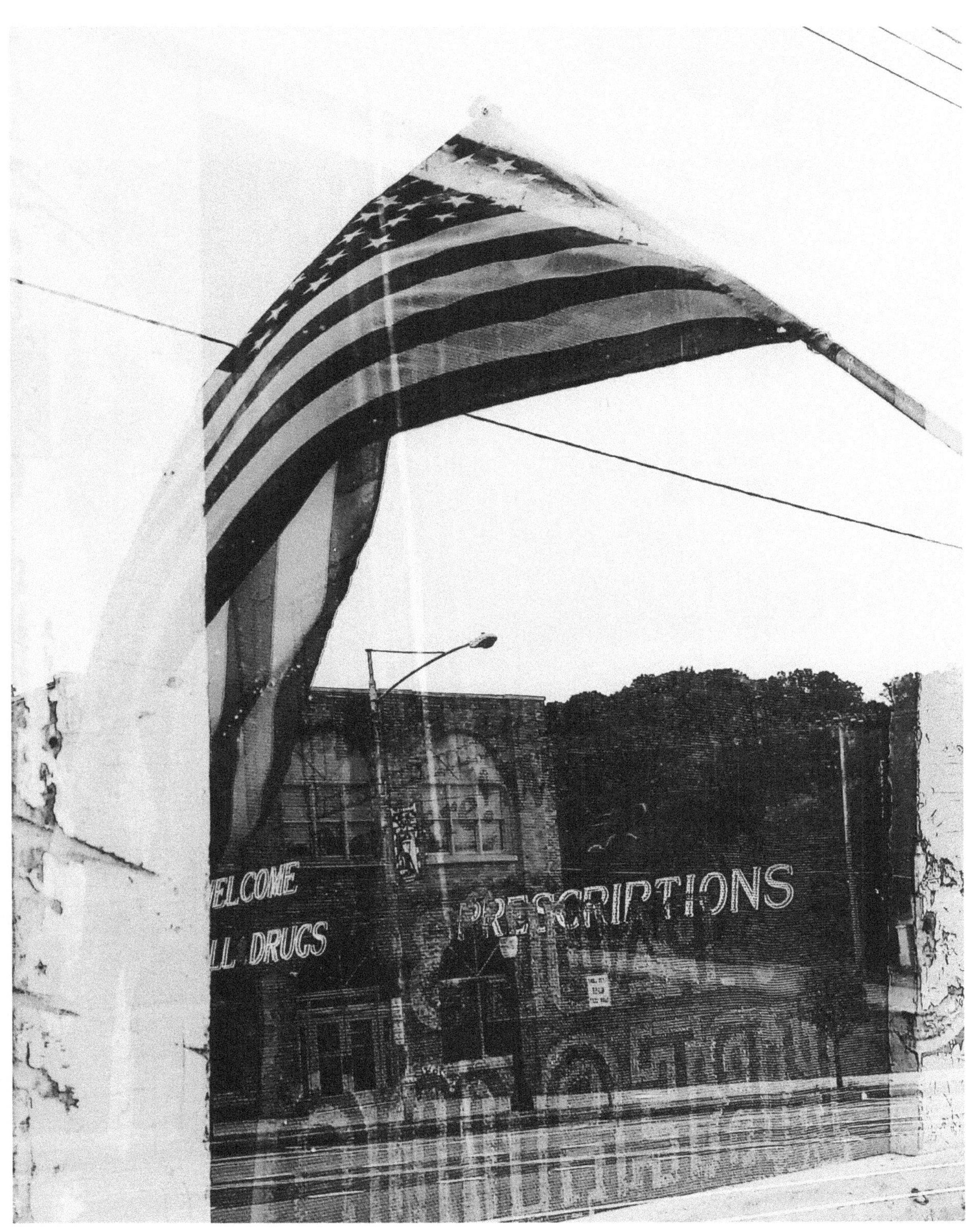

Beaver Falls, PA

1

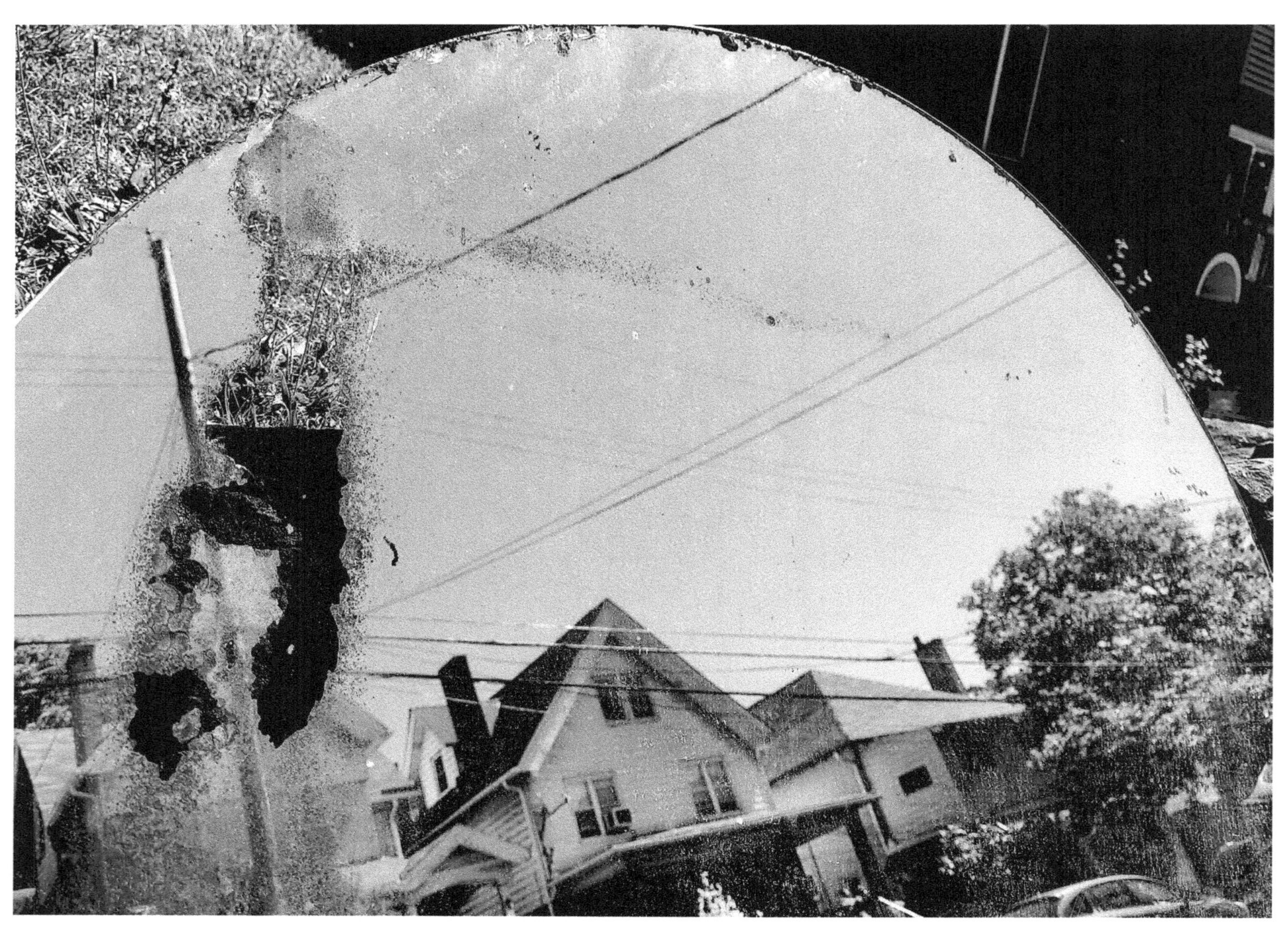

Squirrel Hill, PA

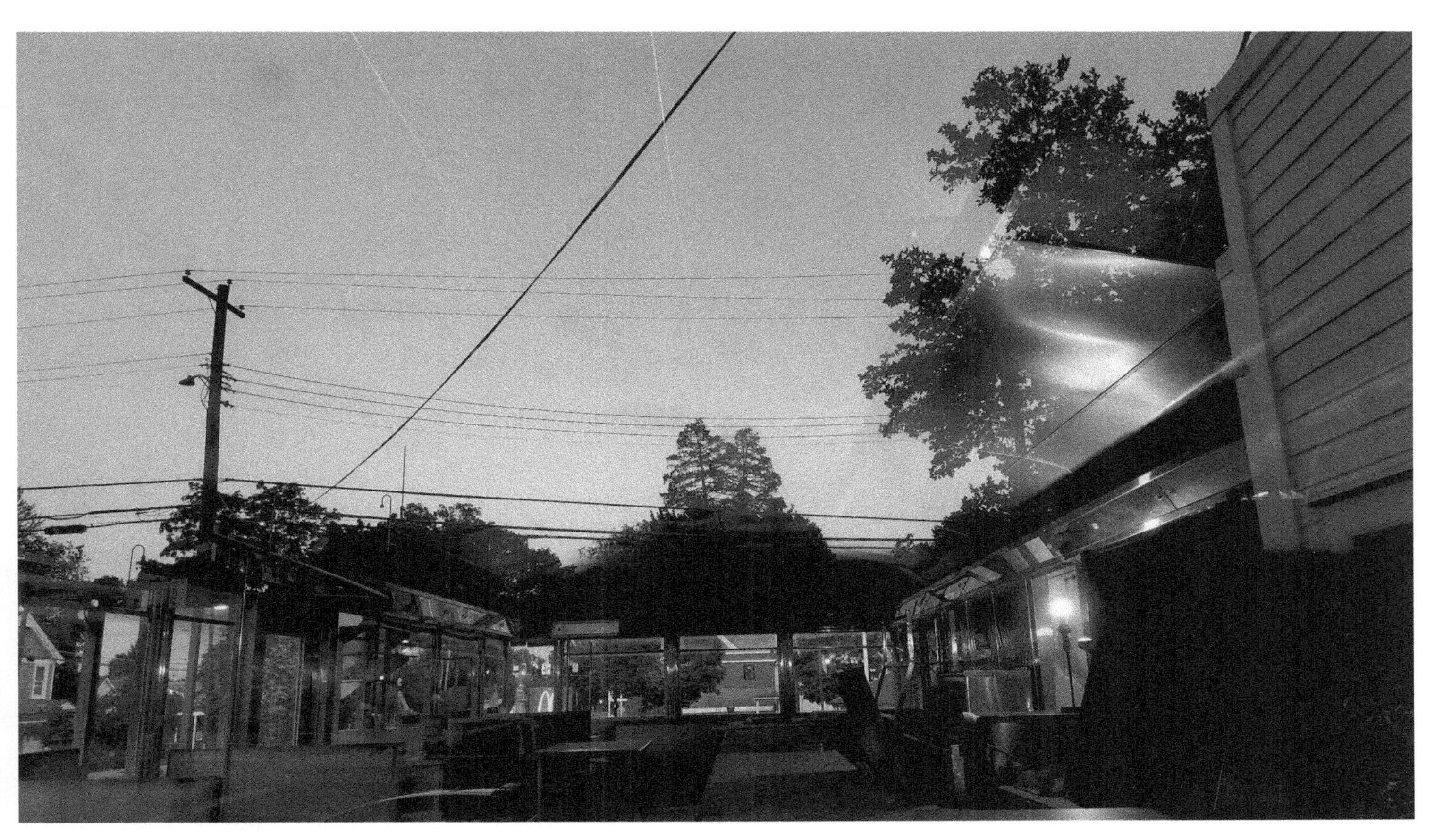

Winchester, VA

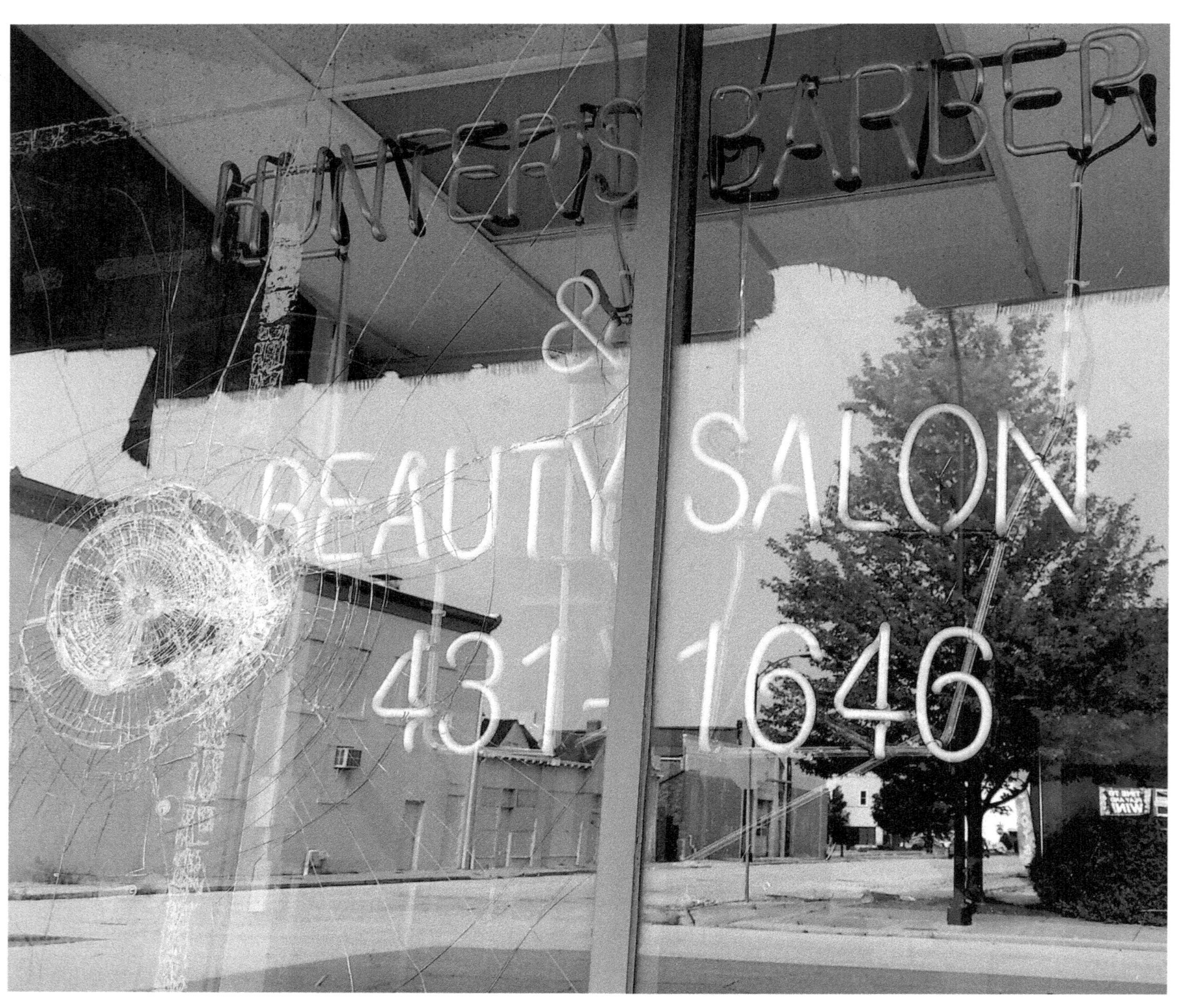

Danville, IL

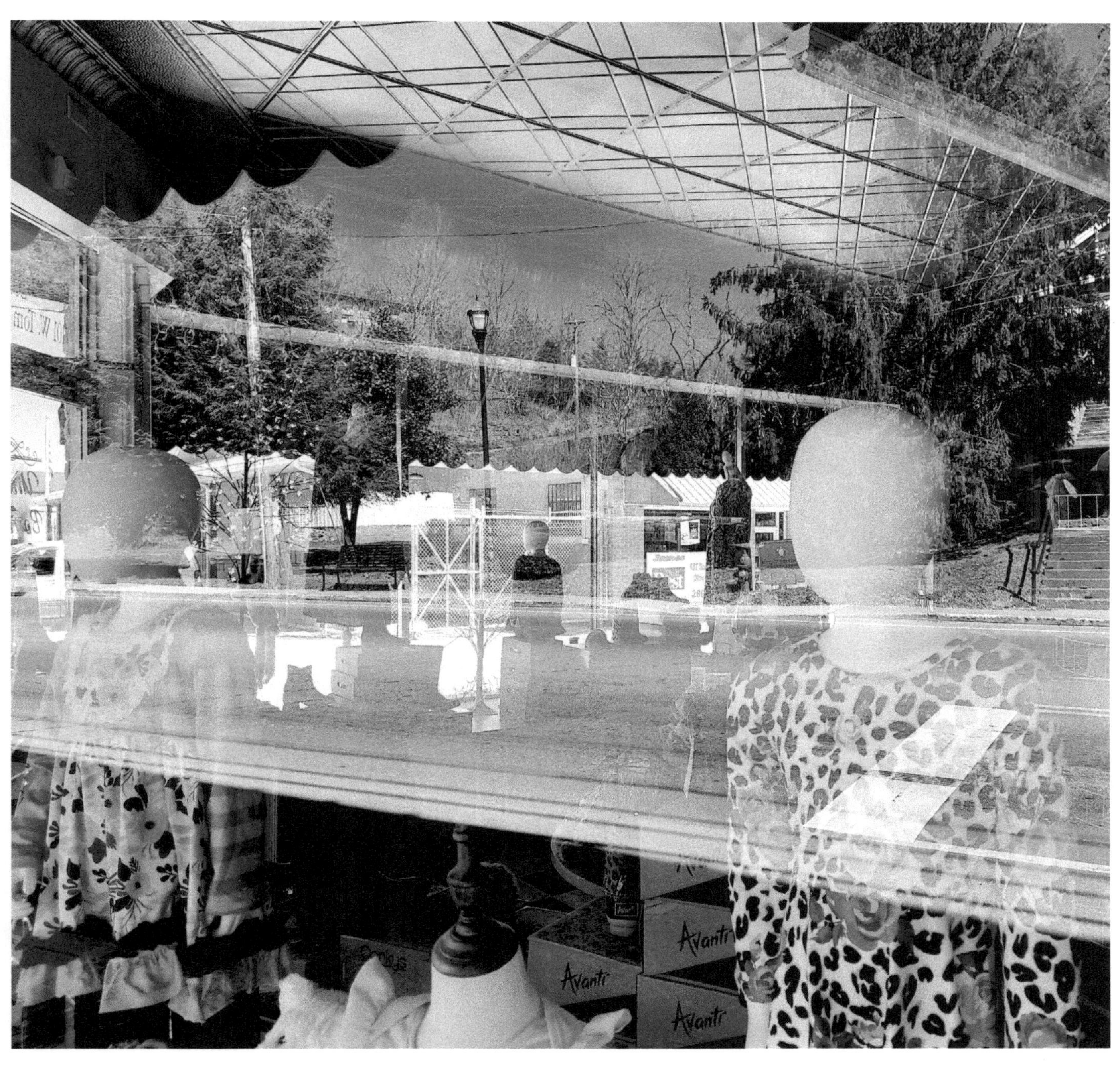

Olive Hill, KY

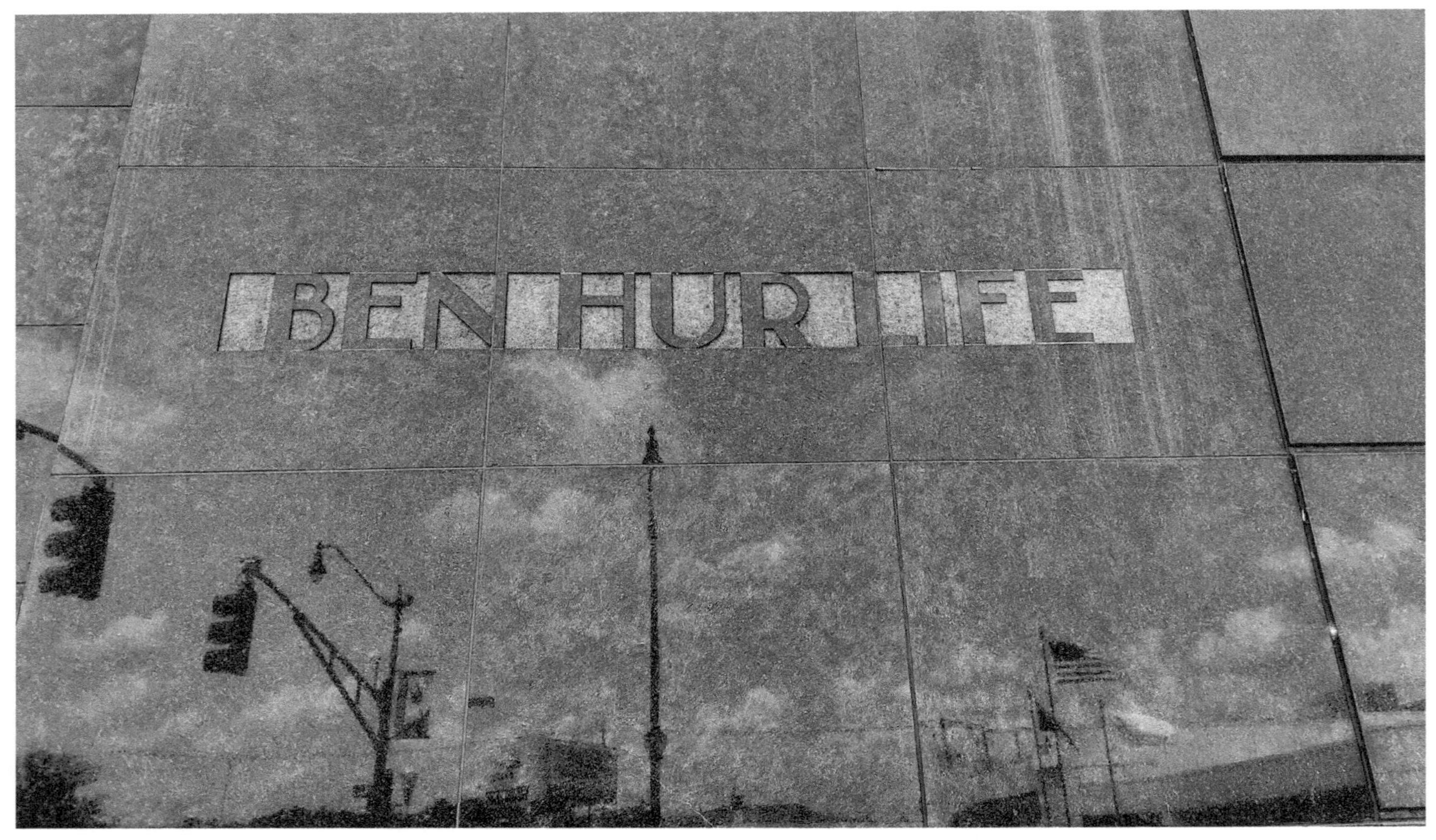

Crawfordsville, IN

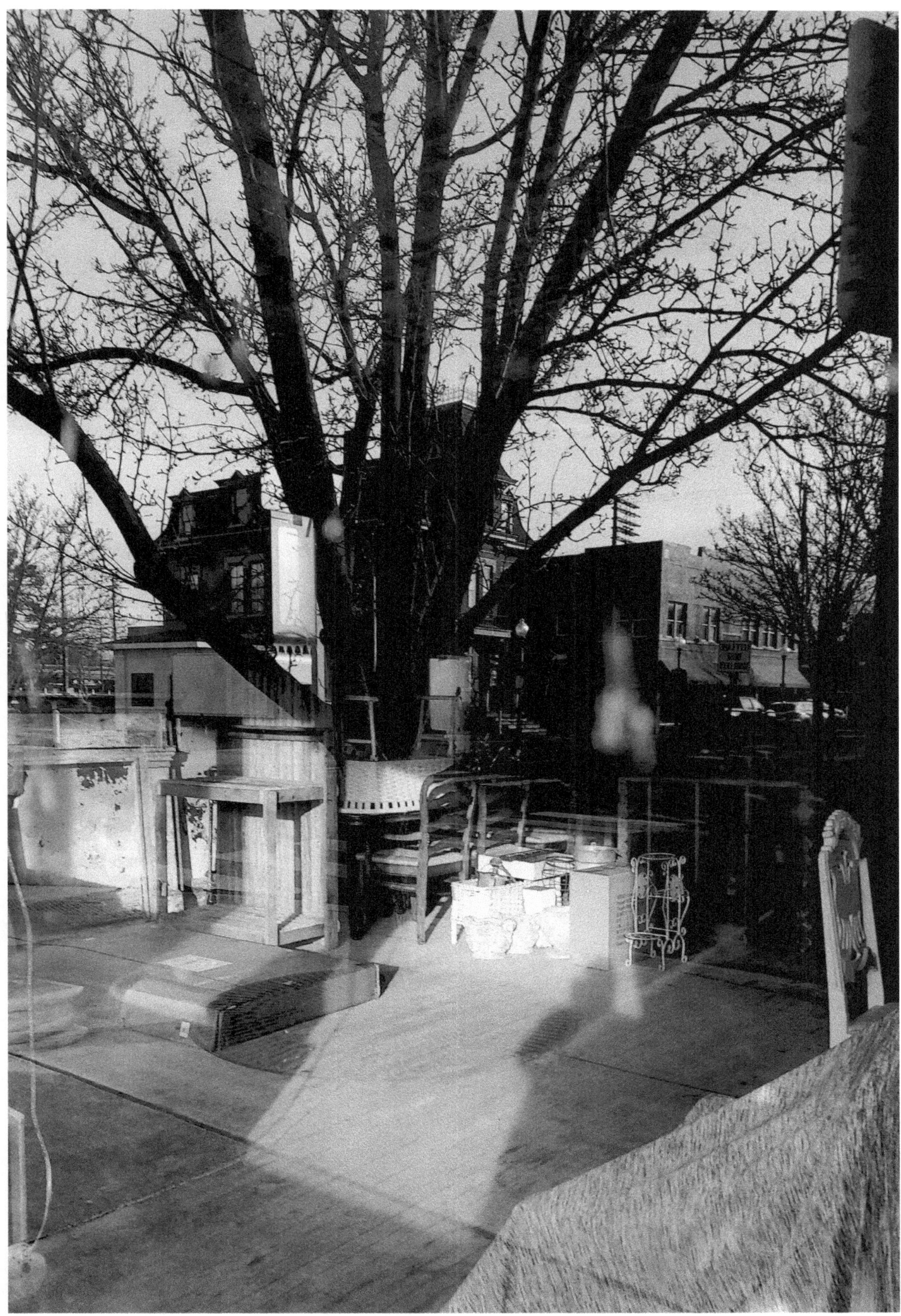

Monroe, MI

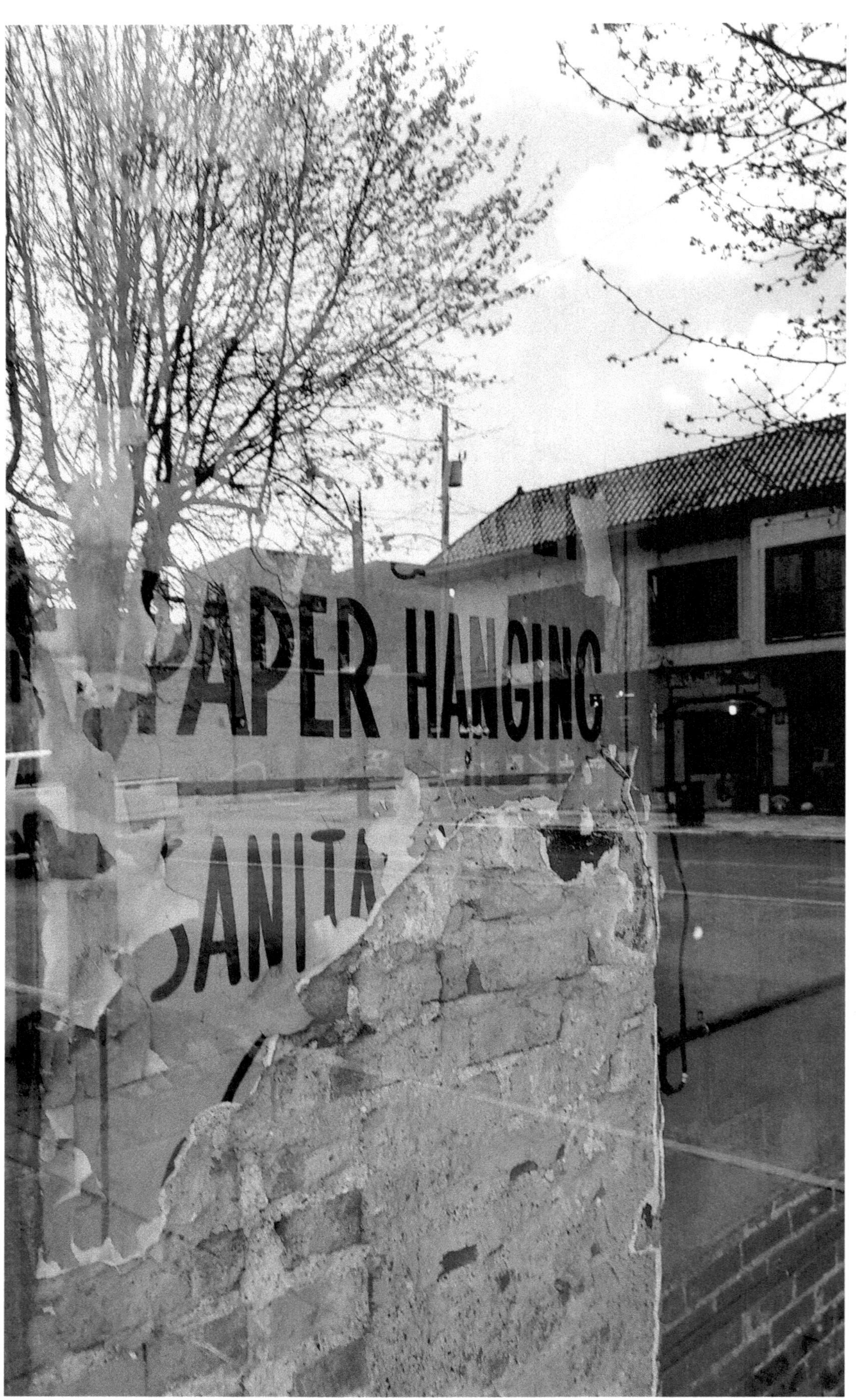

Homestead, PA

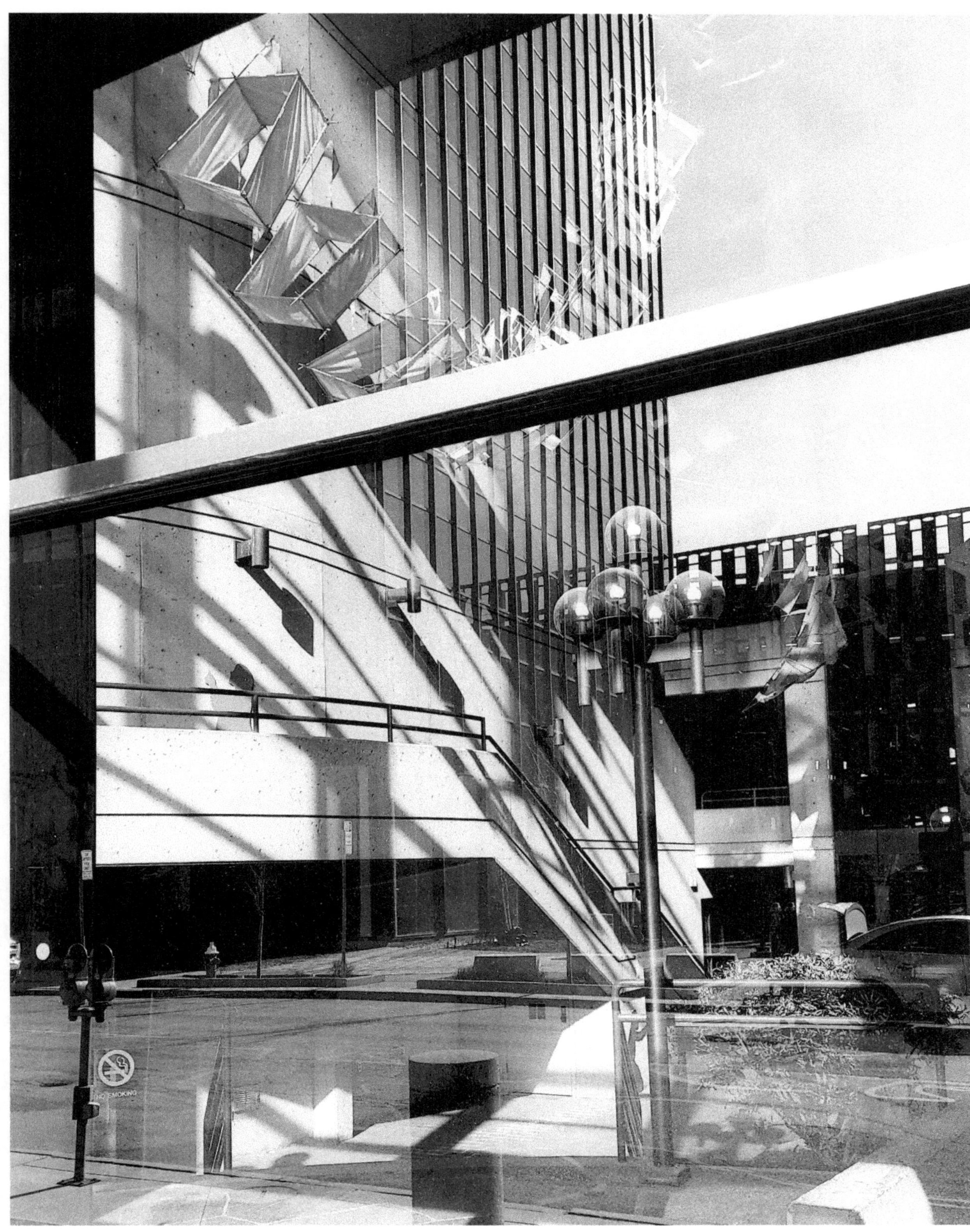

Toledo, OH

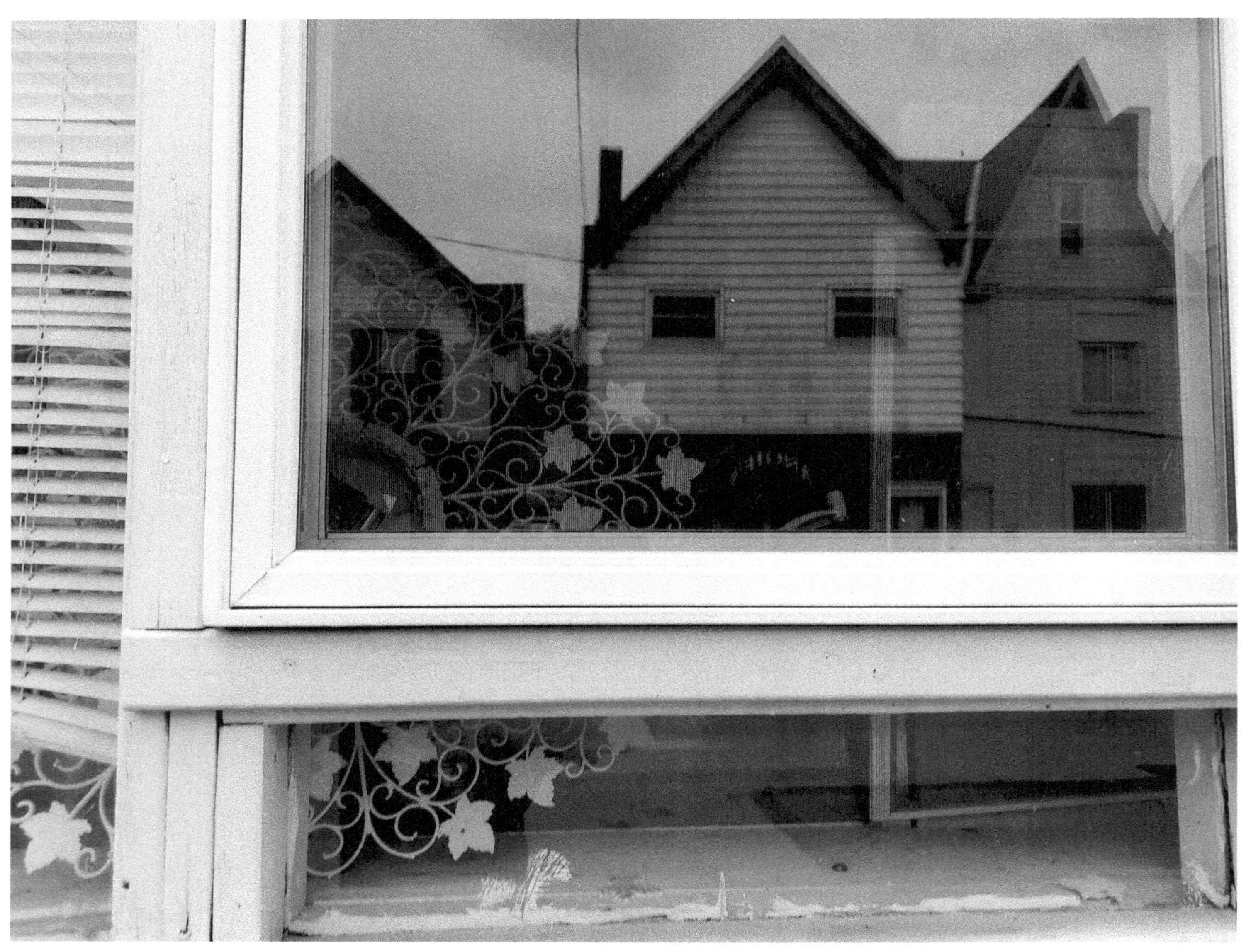

Wilmerding, PA

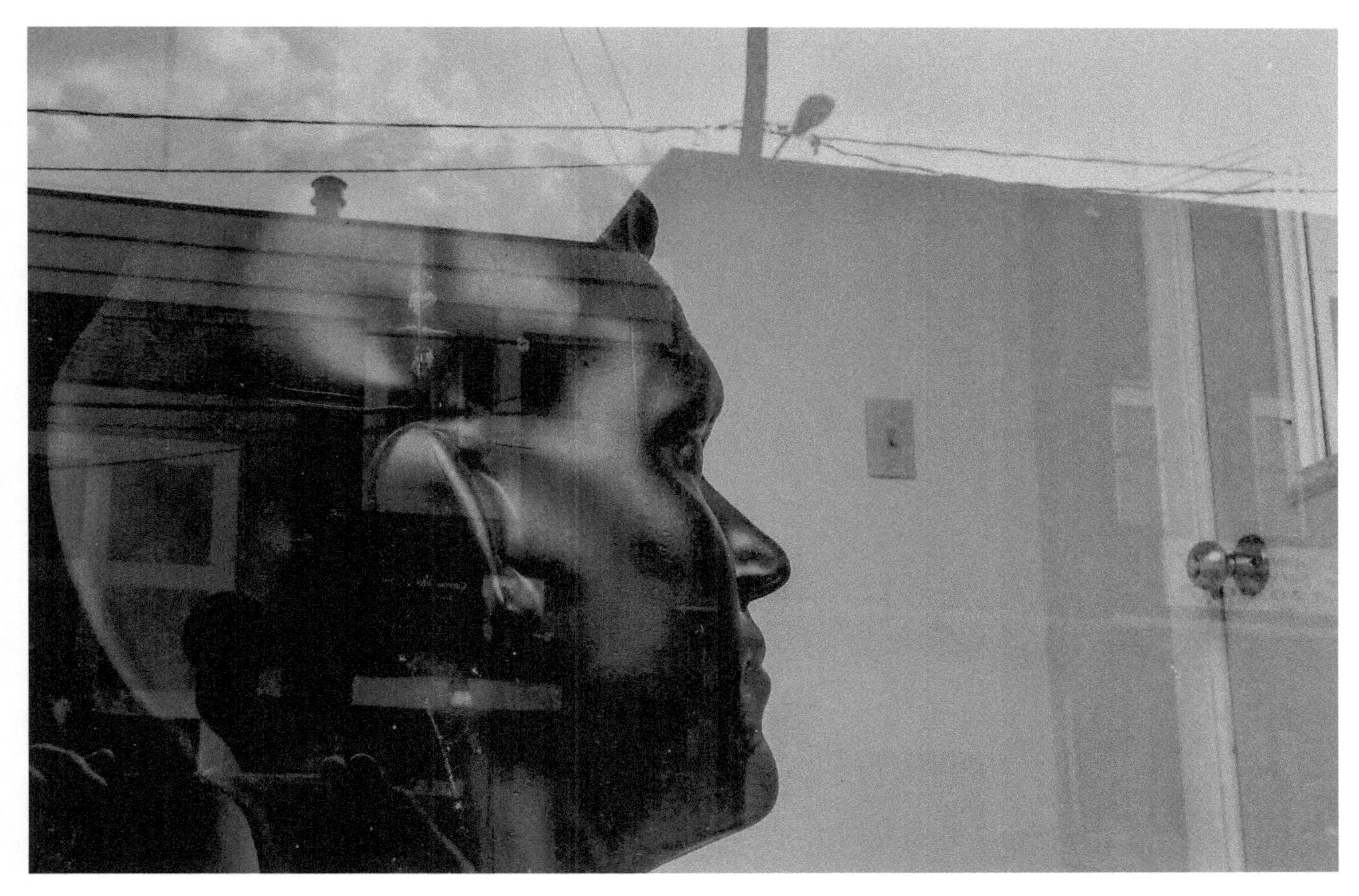

Cambria City, PA

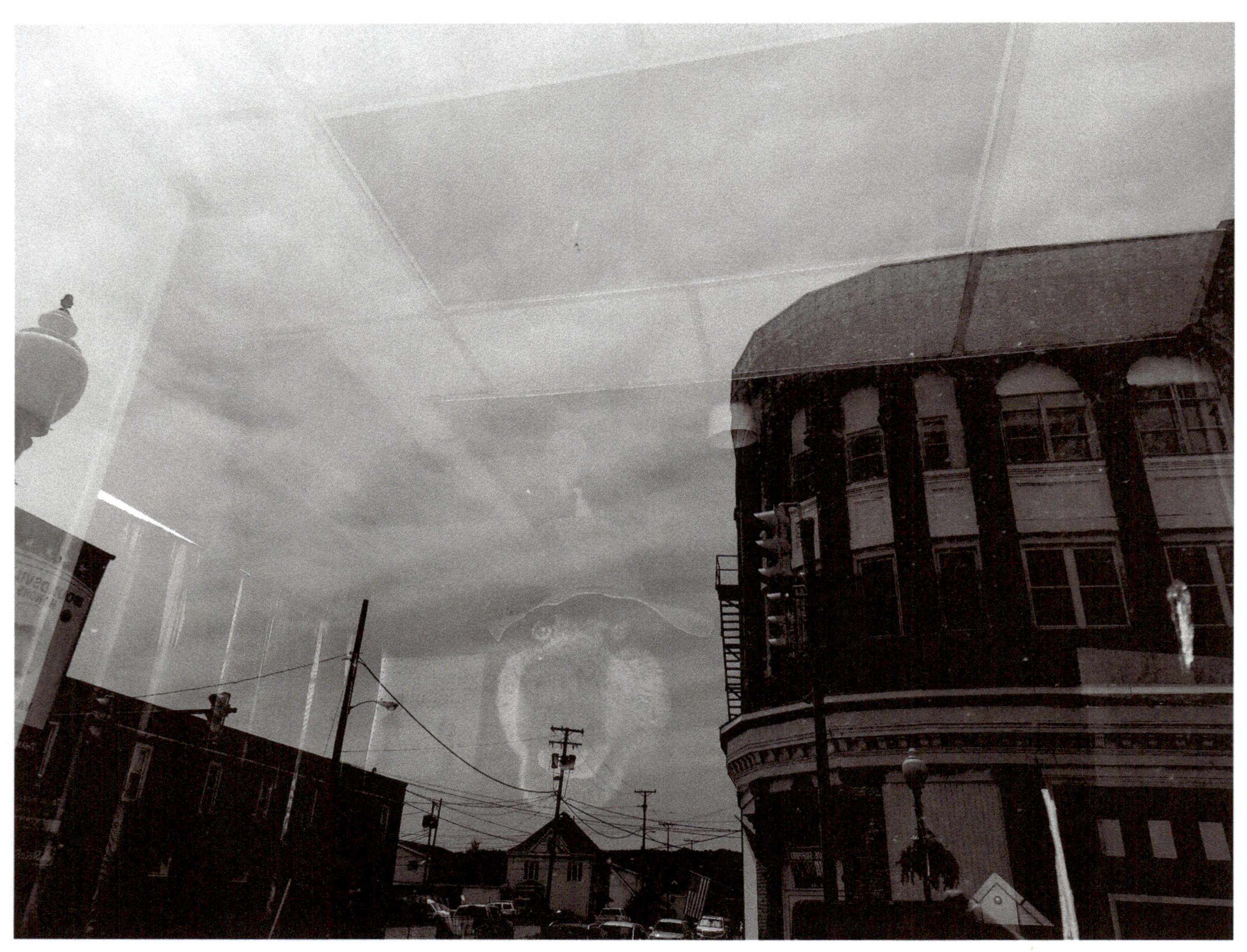

Moundsville, WV

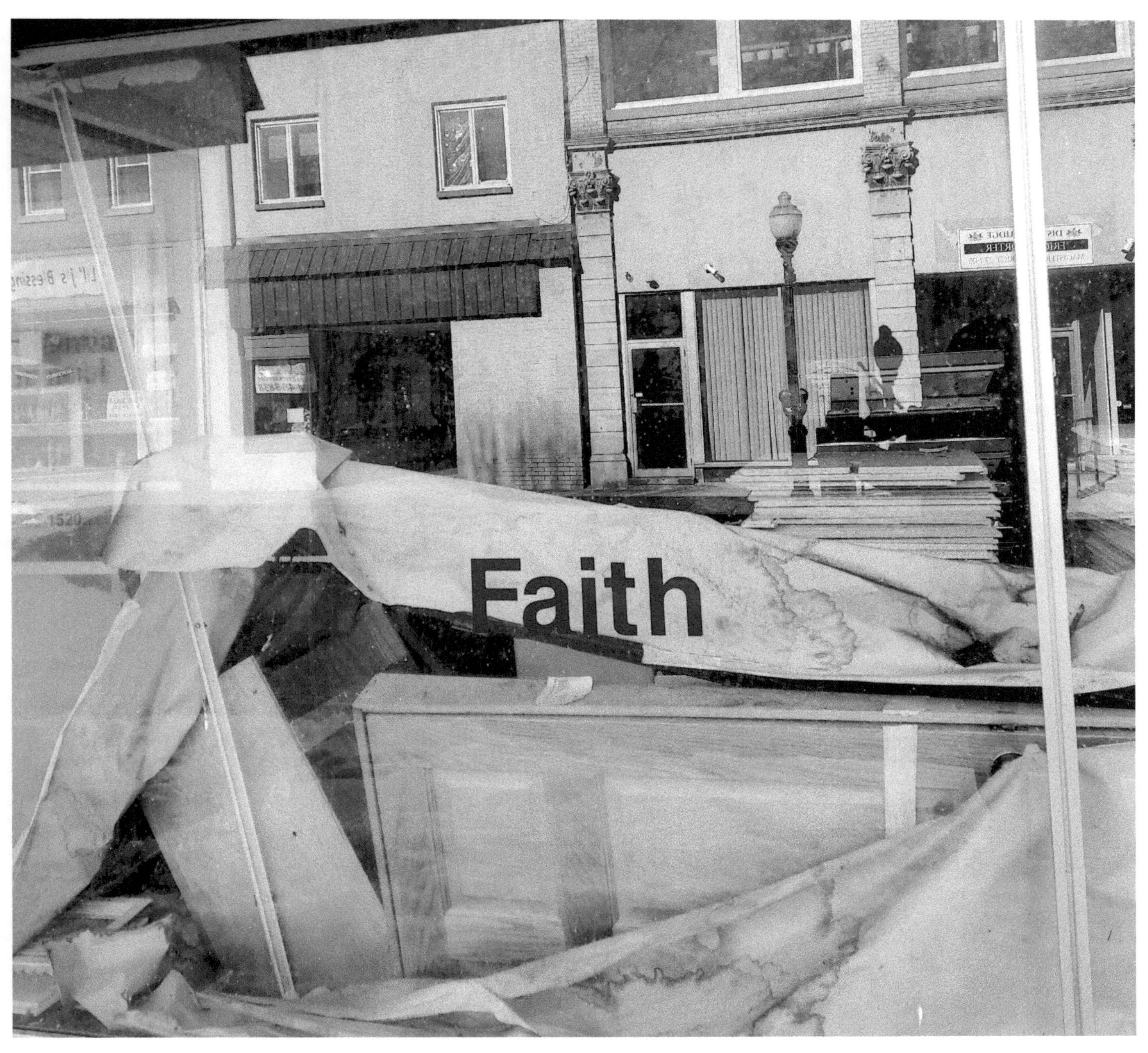

Donora, PA

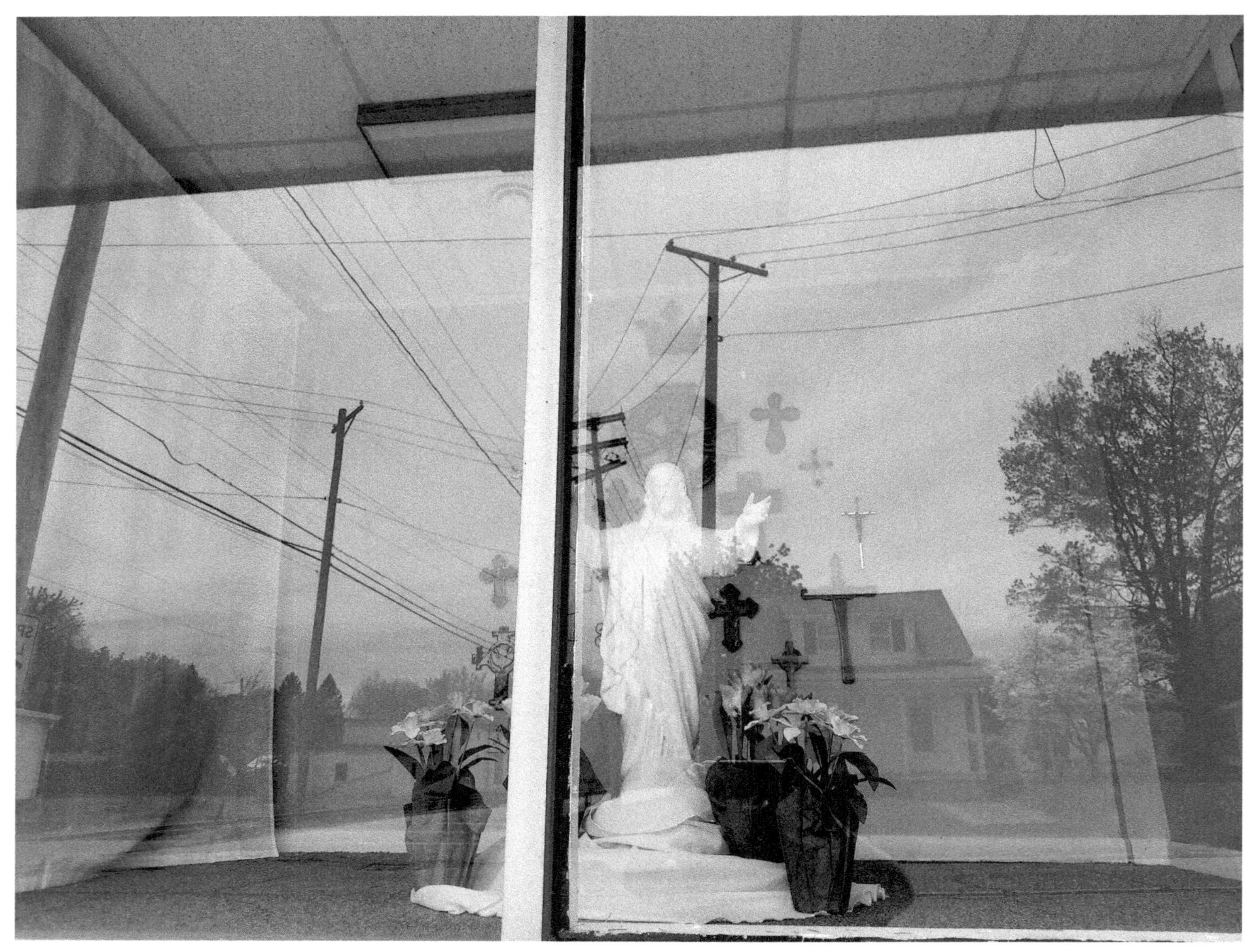

Columbiana, OH

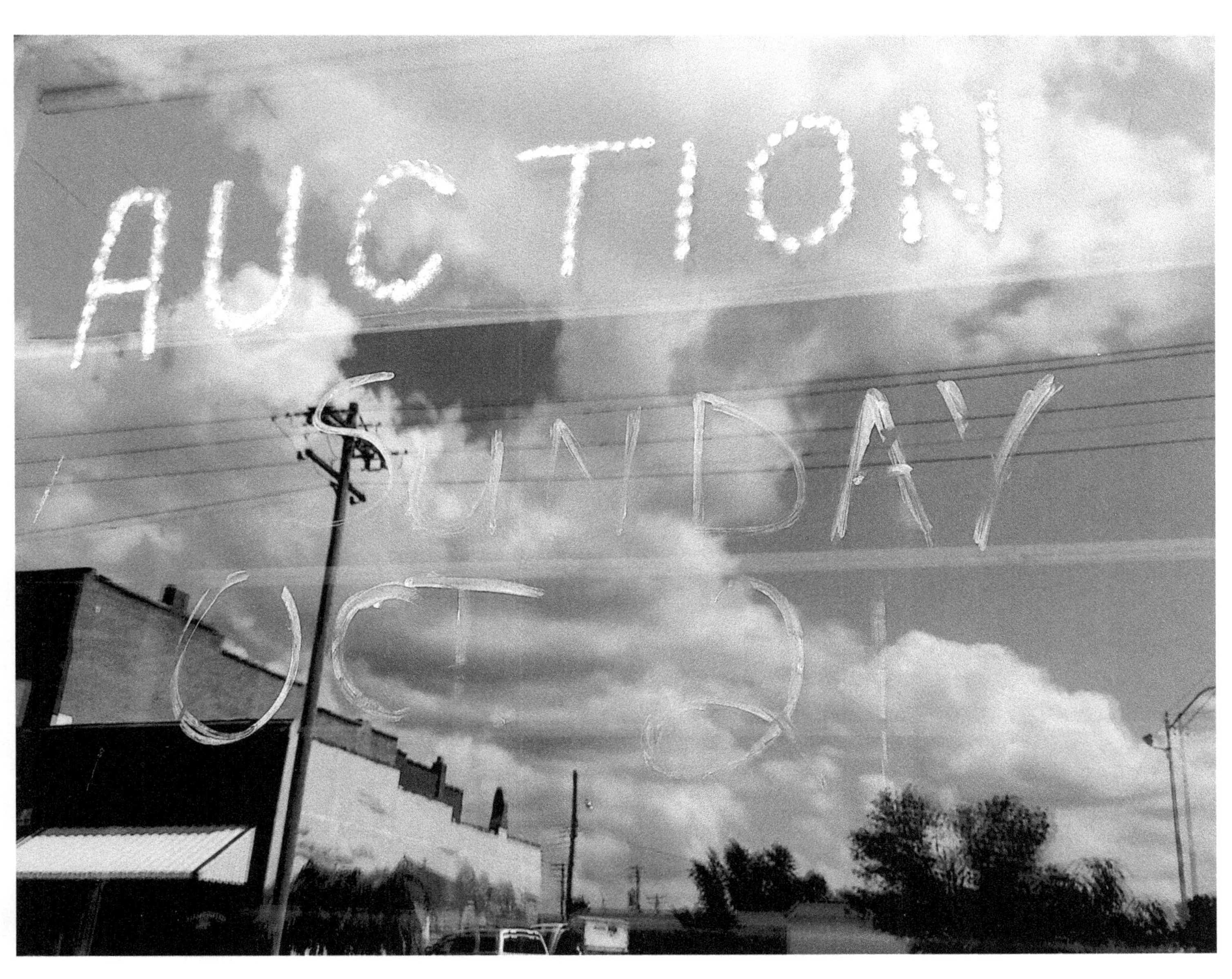

Montgomery City, MO

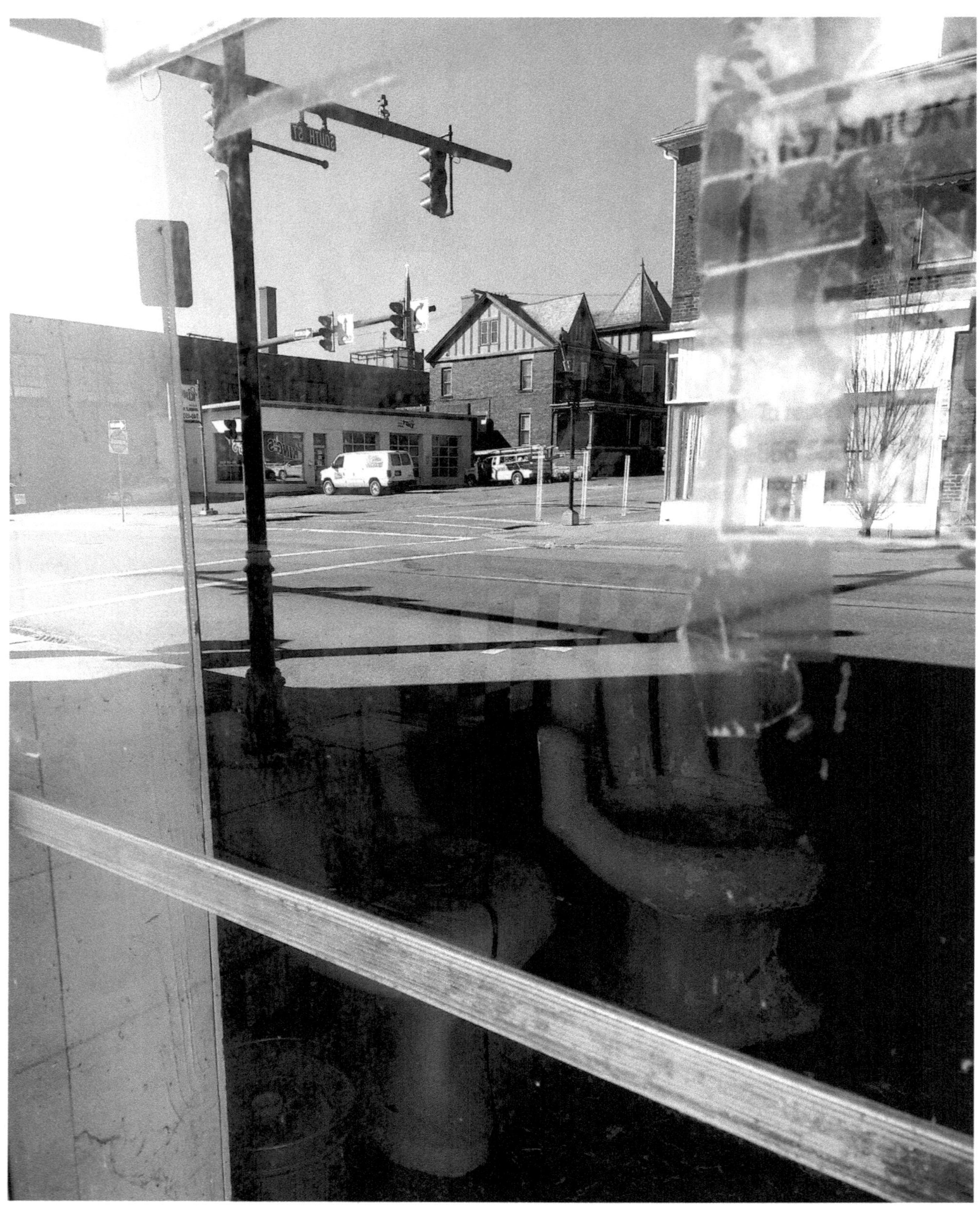

Zanesville, OH

16

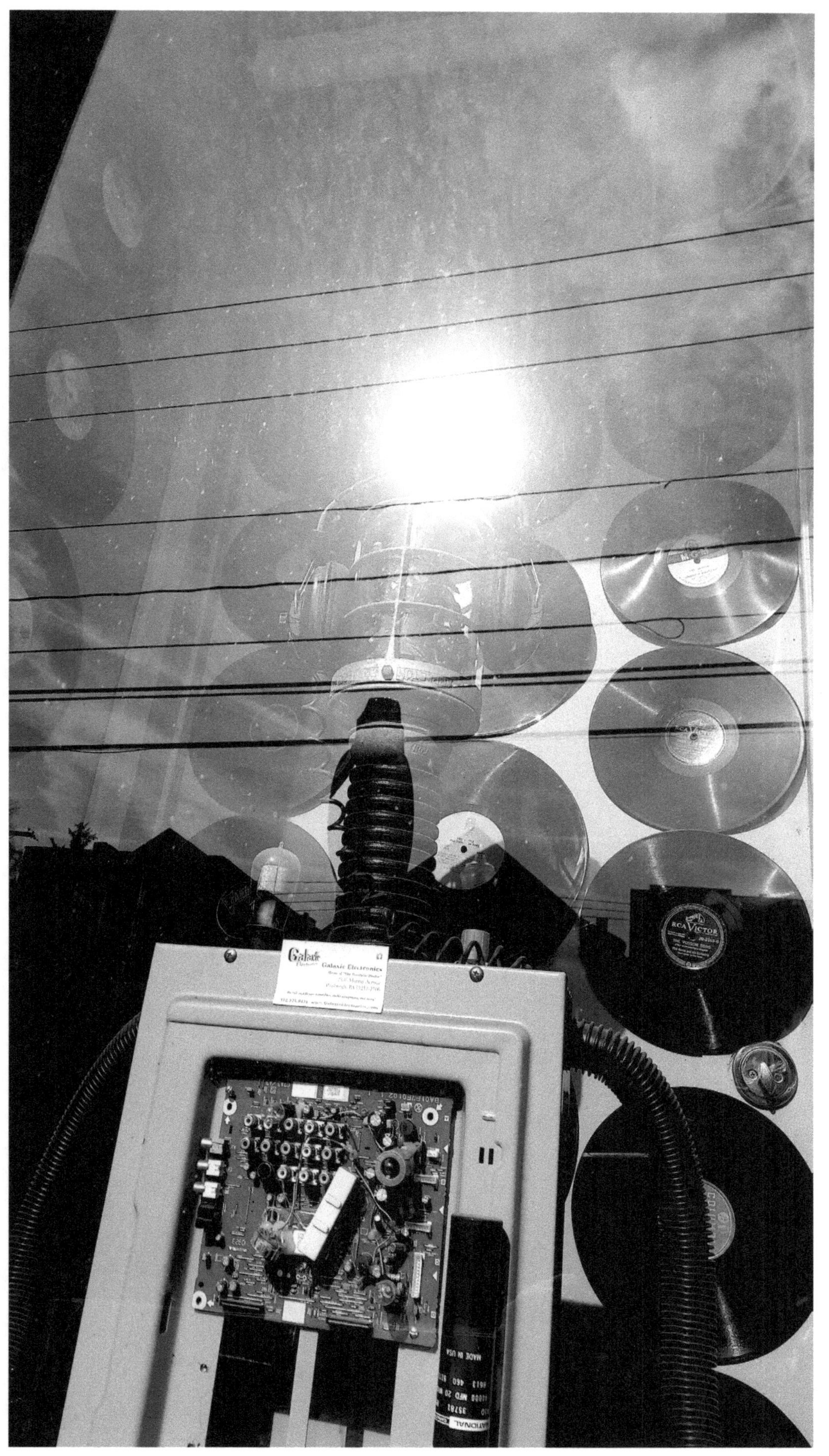

Squirrel Hill, PA

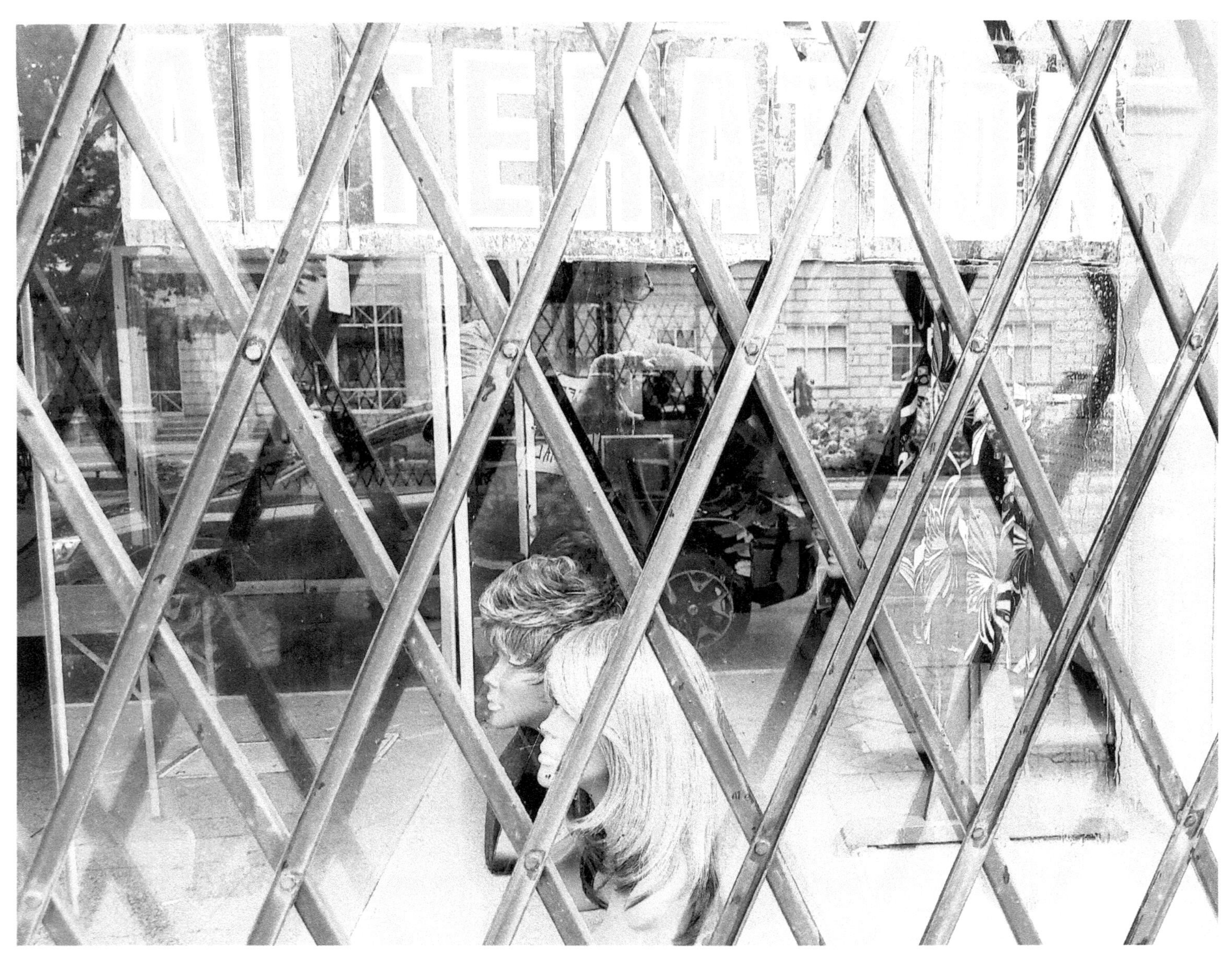

Youngstown, OH

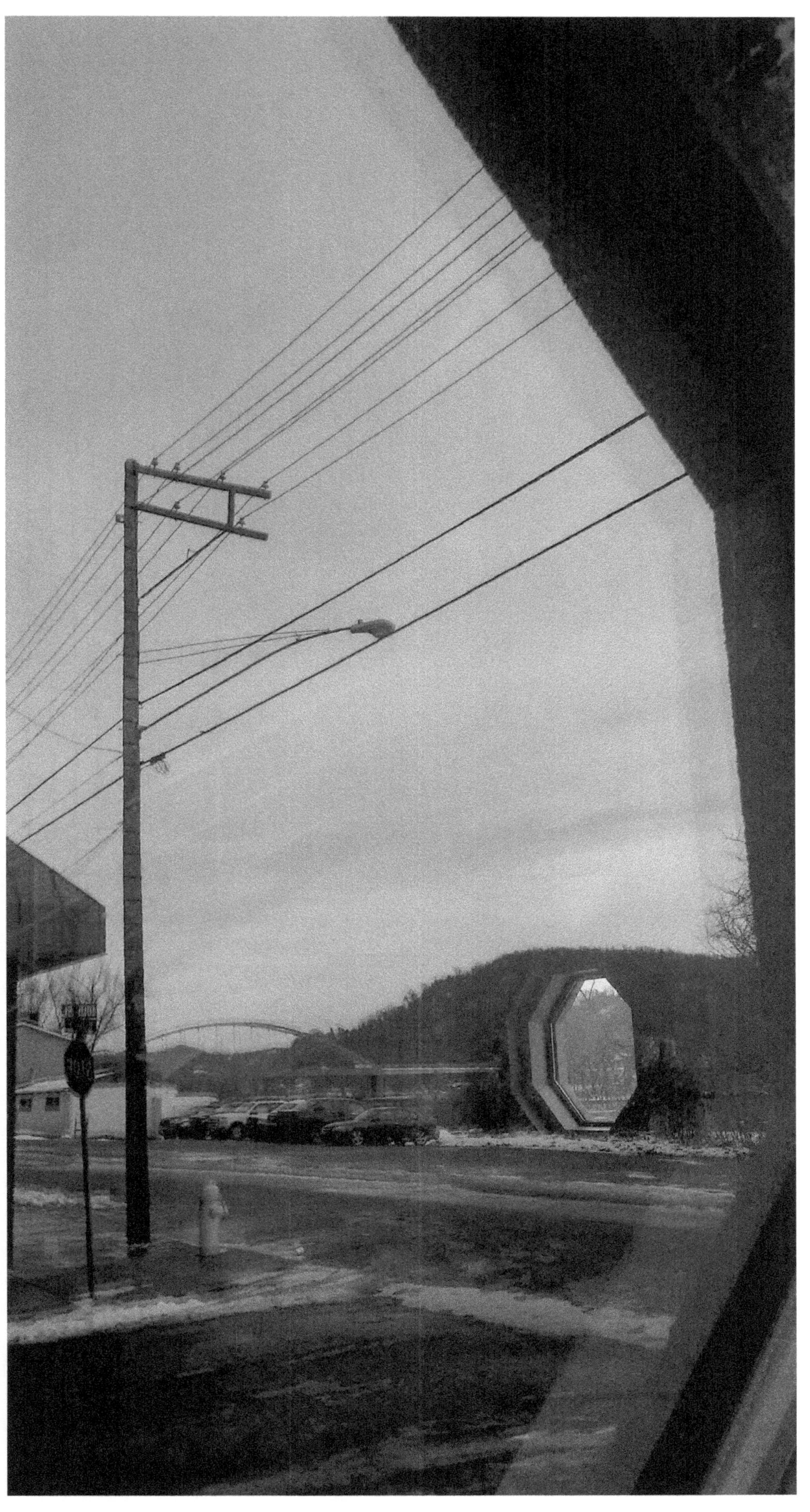

Benwood, WV

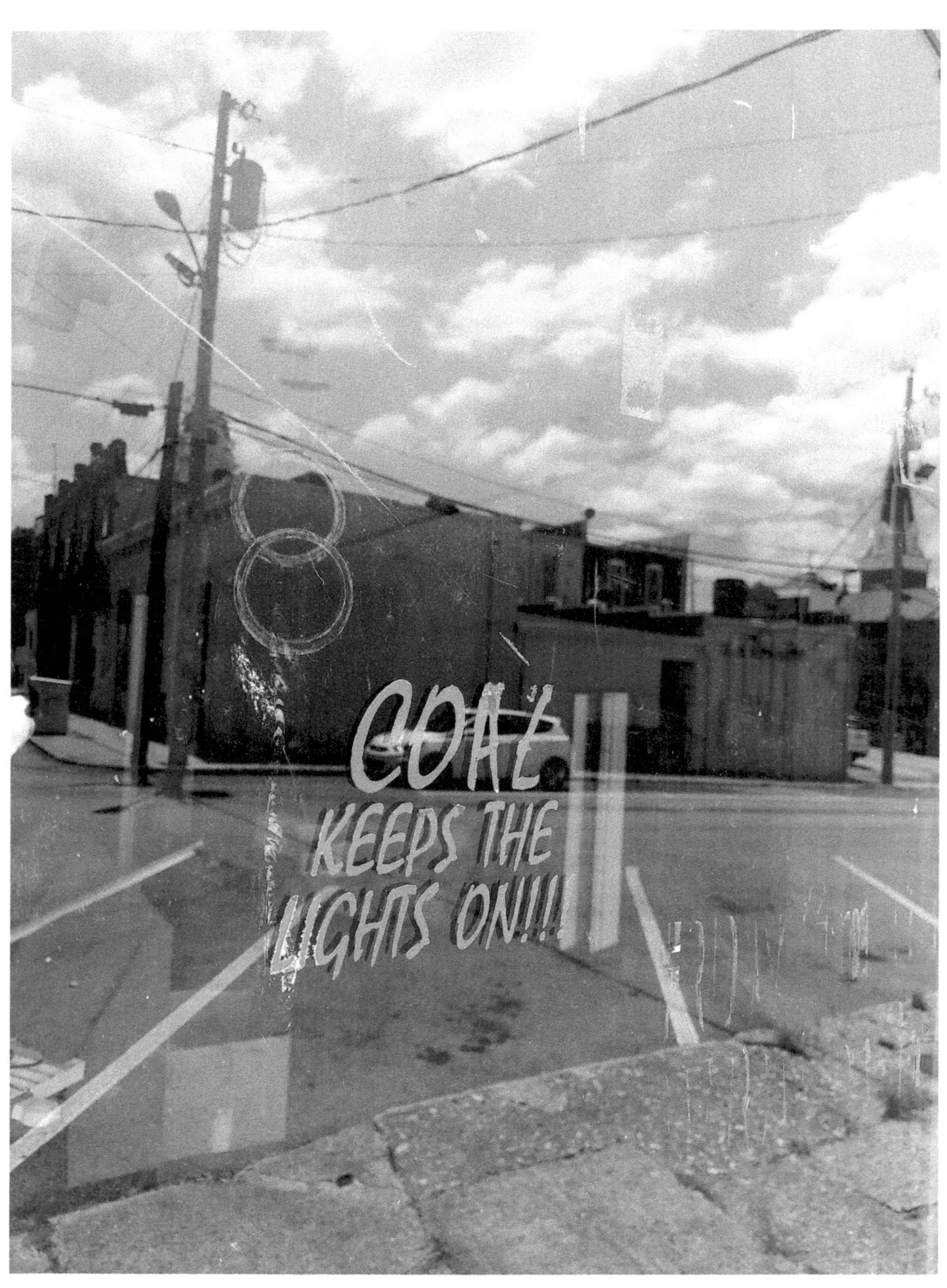

Owingsville, KY

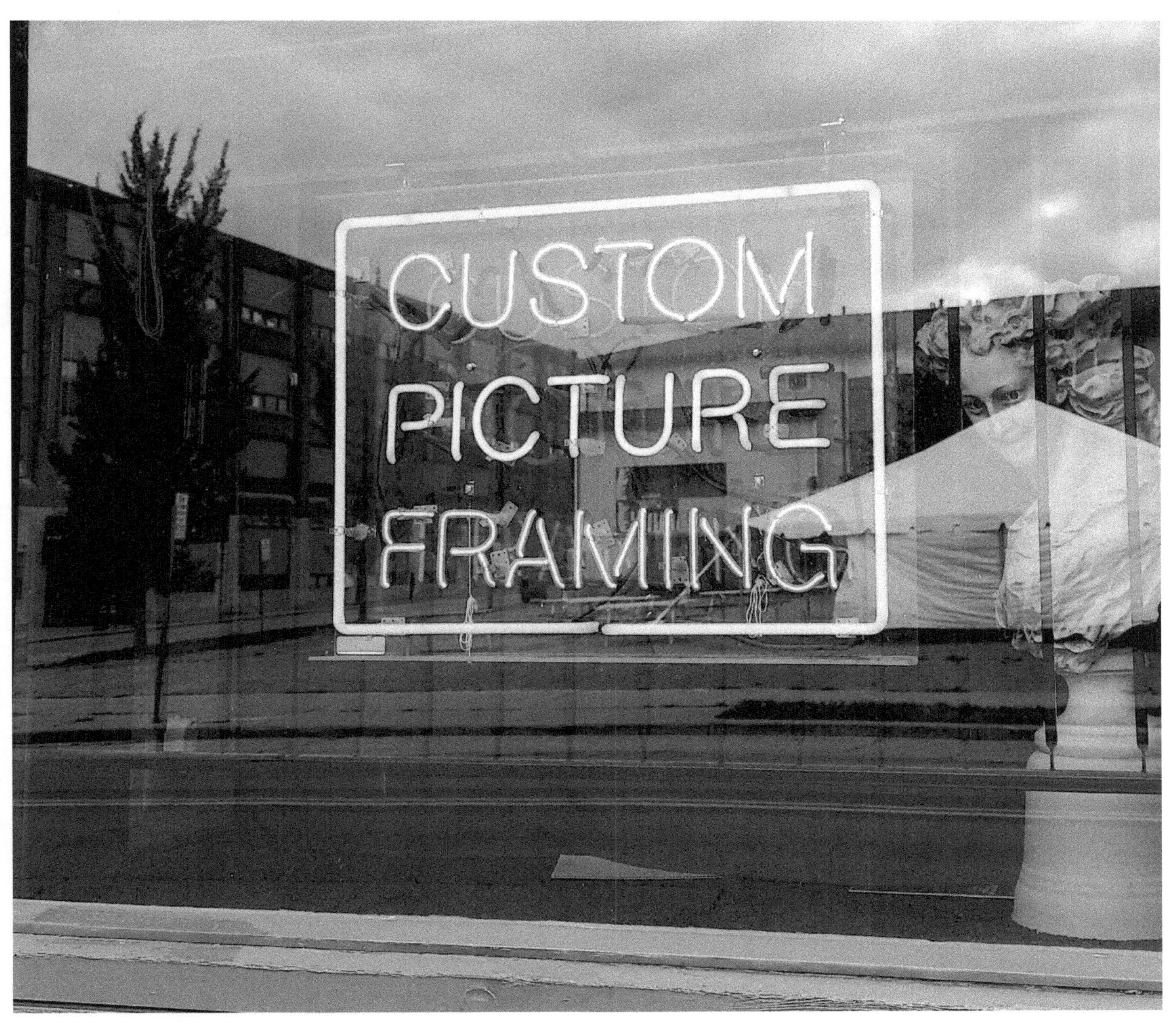

Toledo, OH

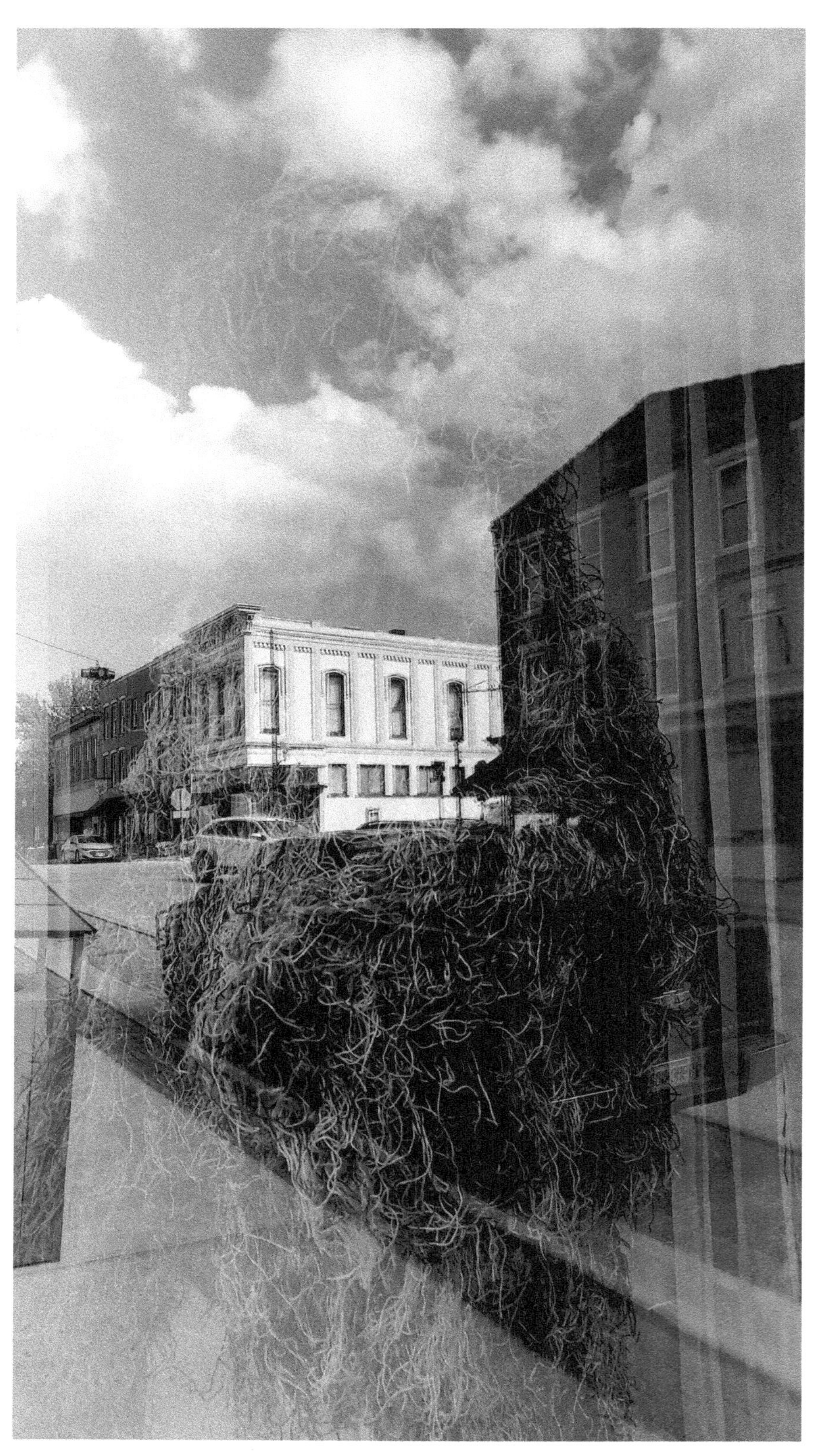

Louisiana, MO

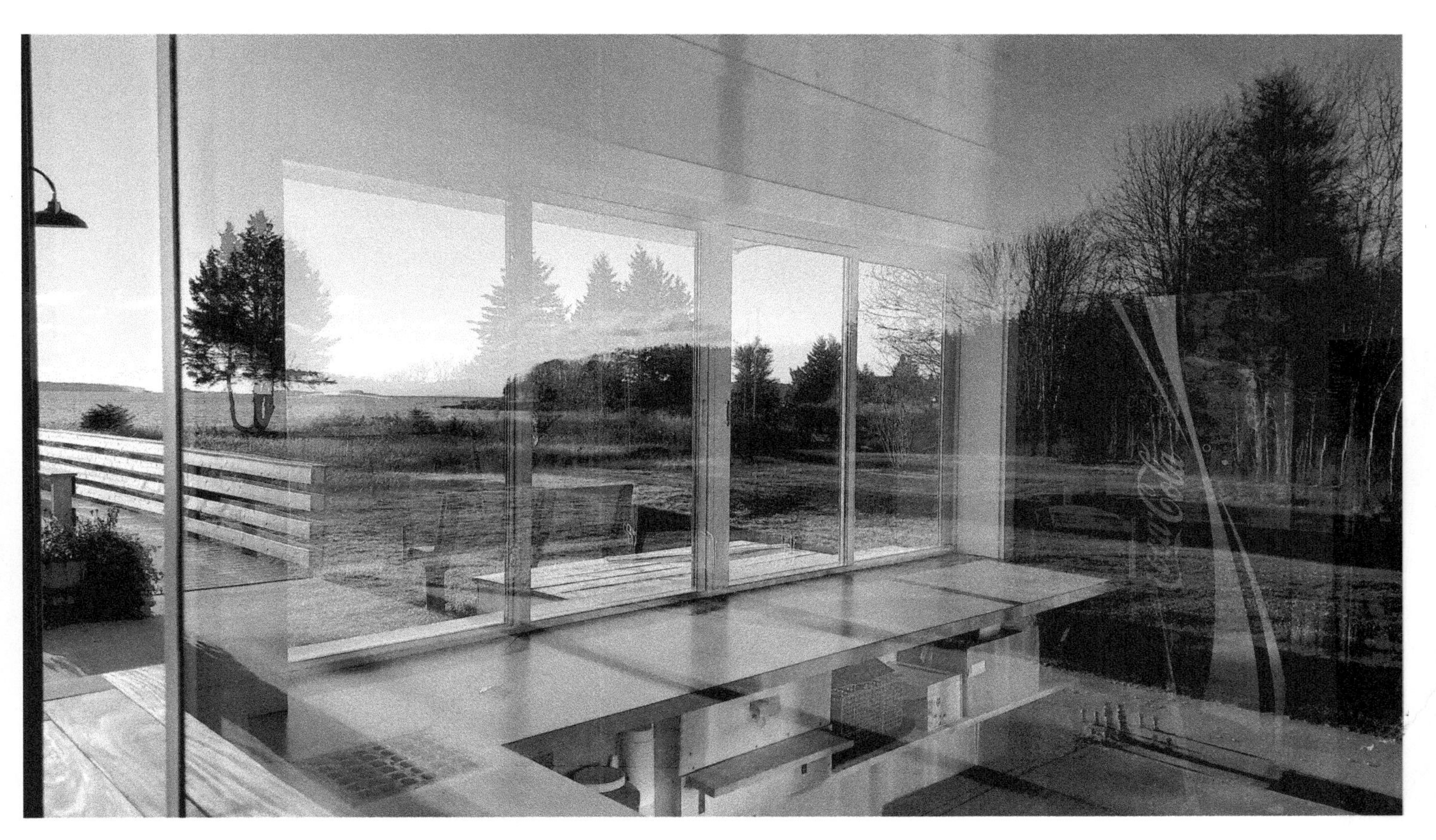

Pemaquid Point, ME

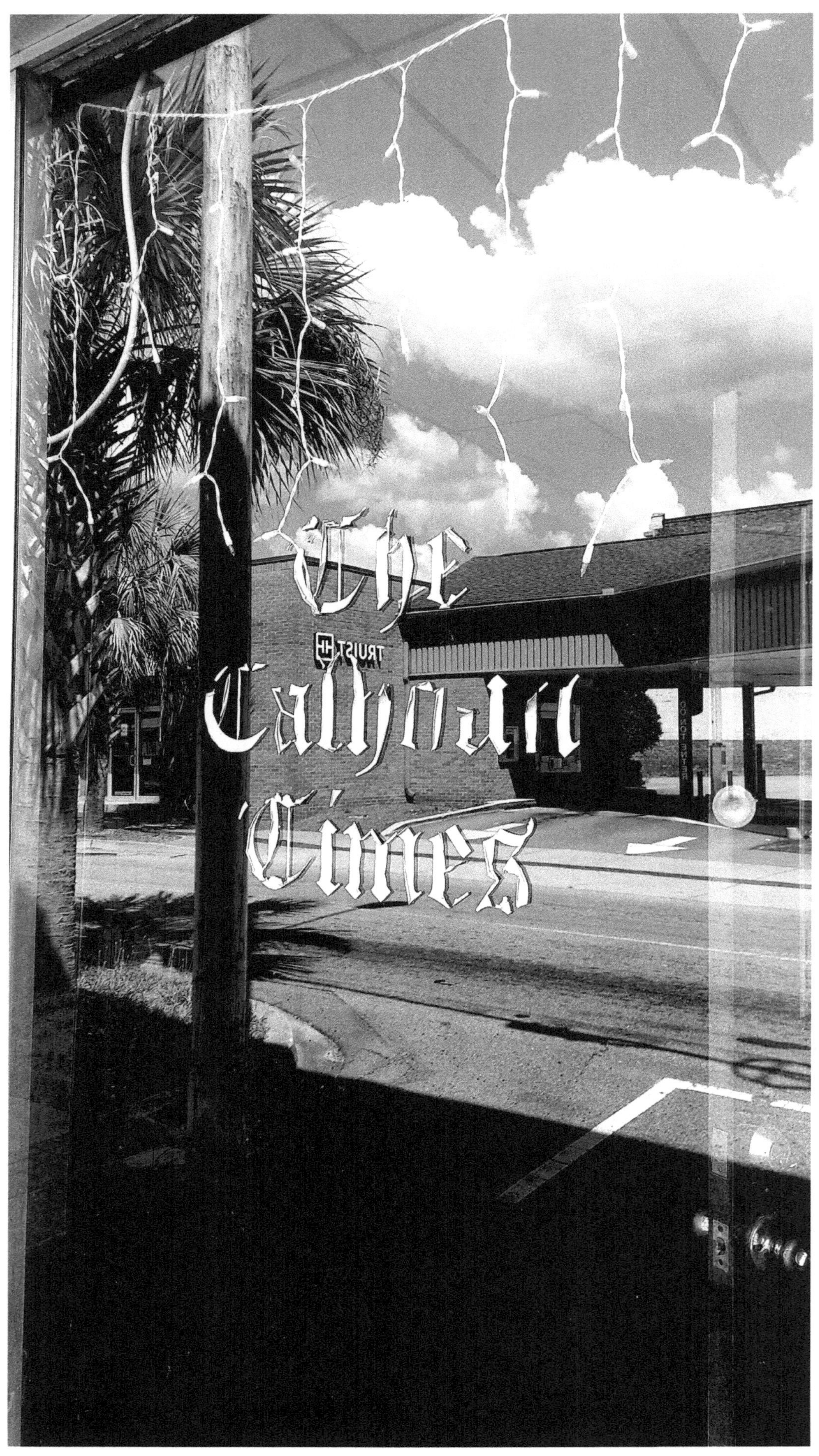

St Matthews, SC

24

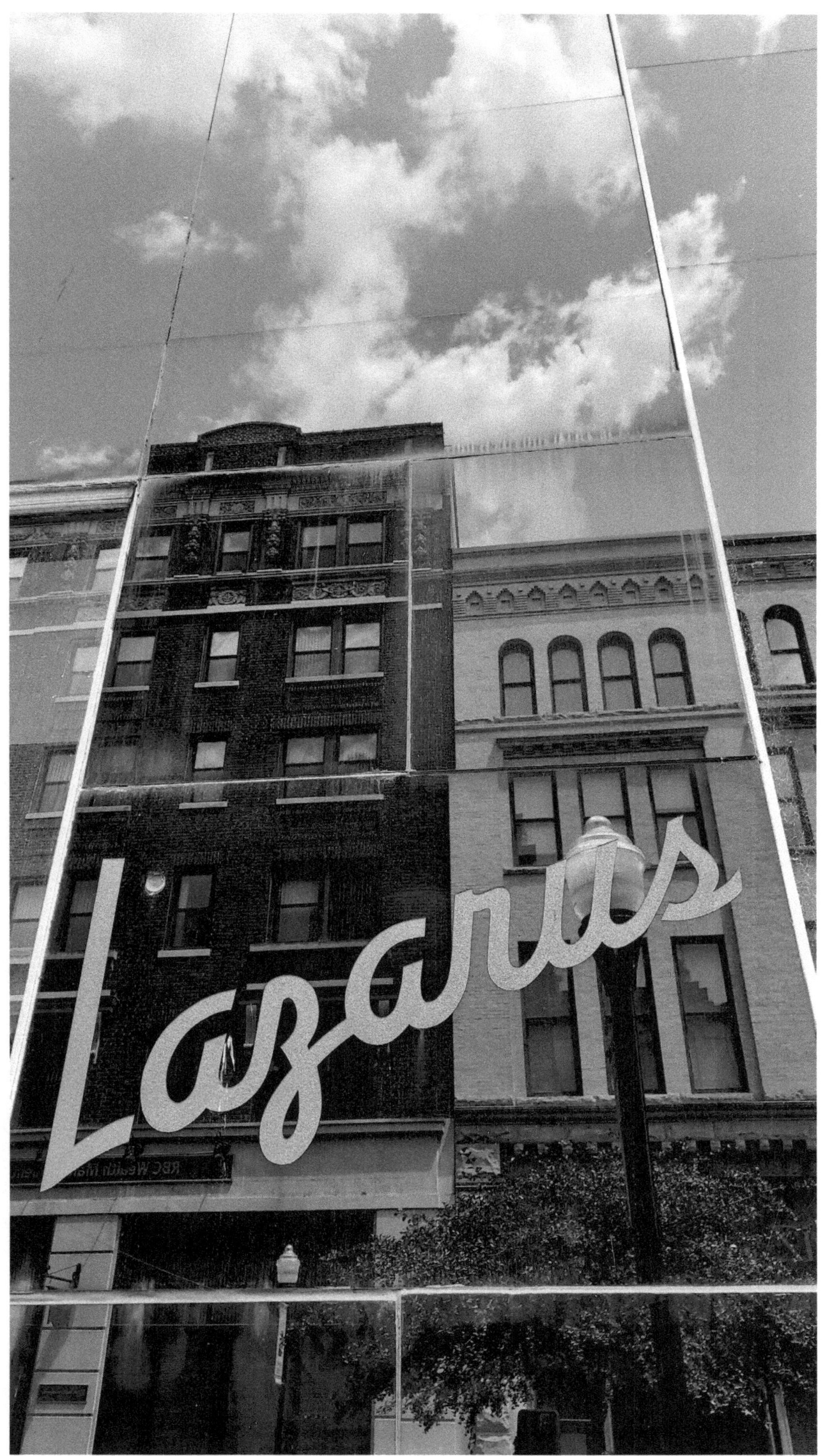

Cumberland, MD

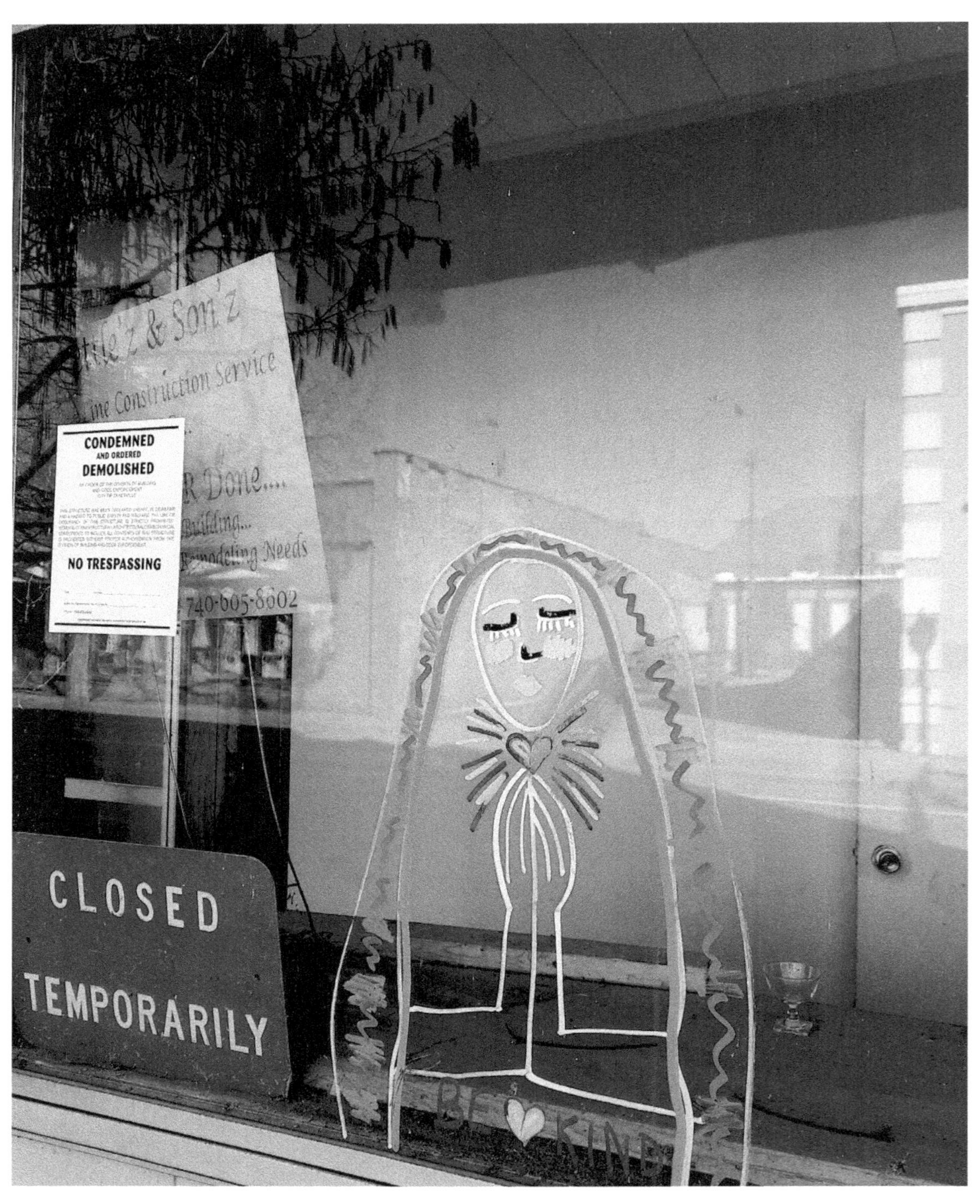

Zanesville, OH

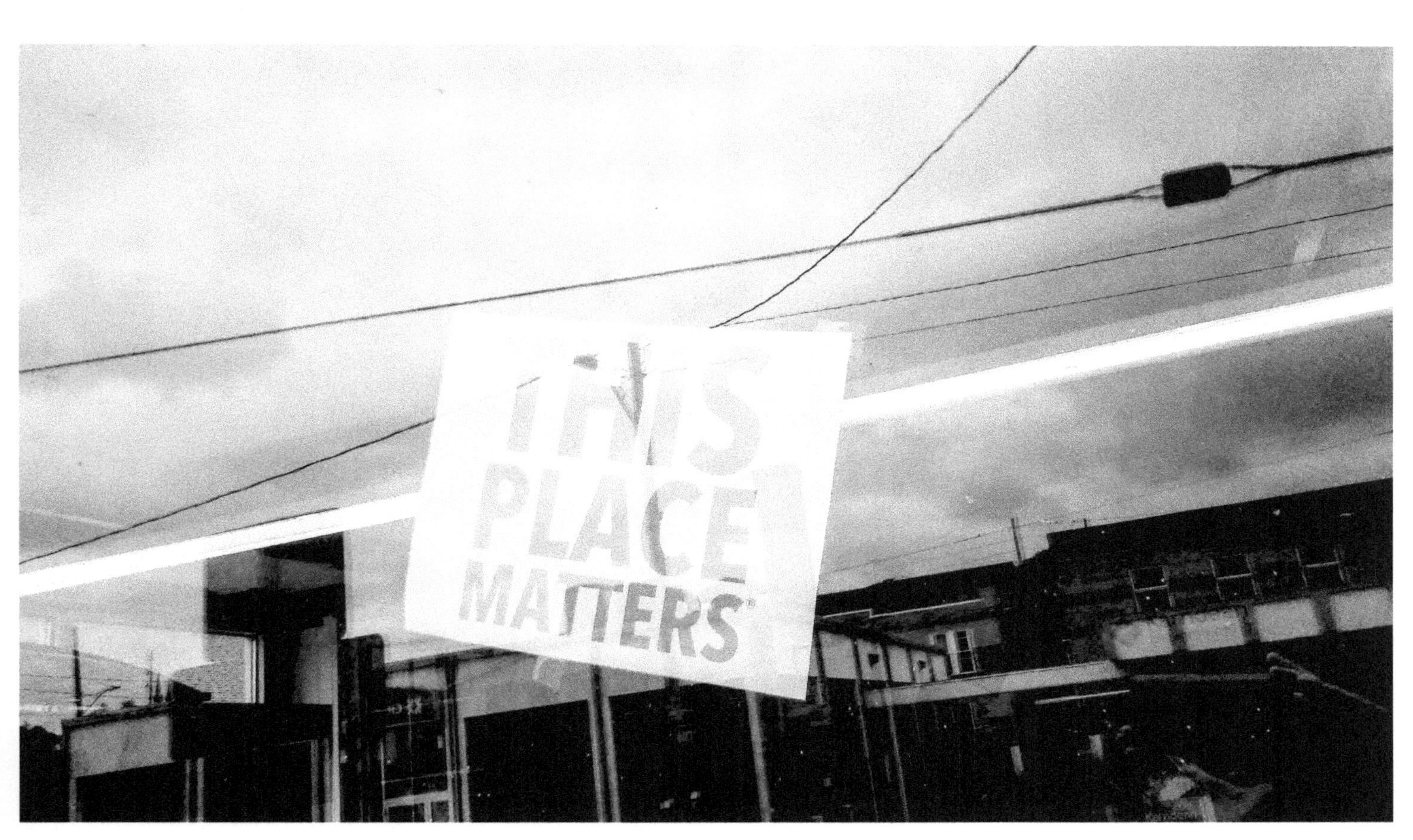

Oil City, PA

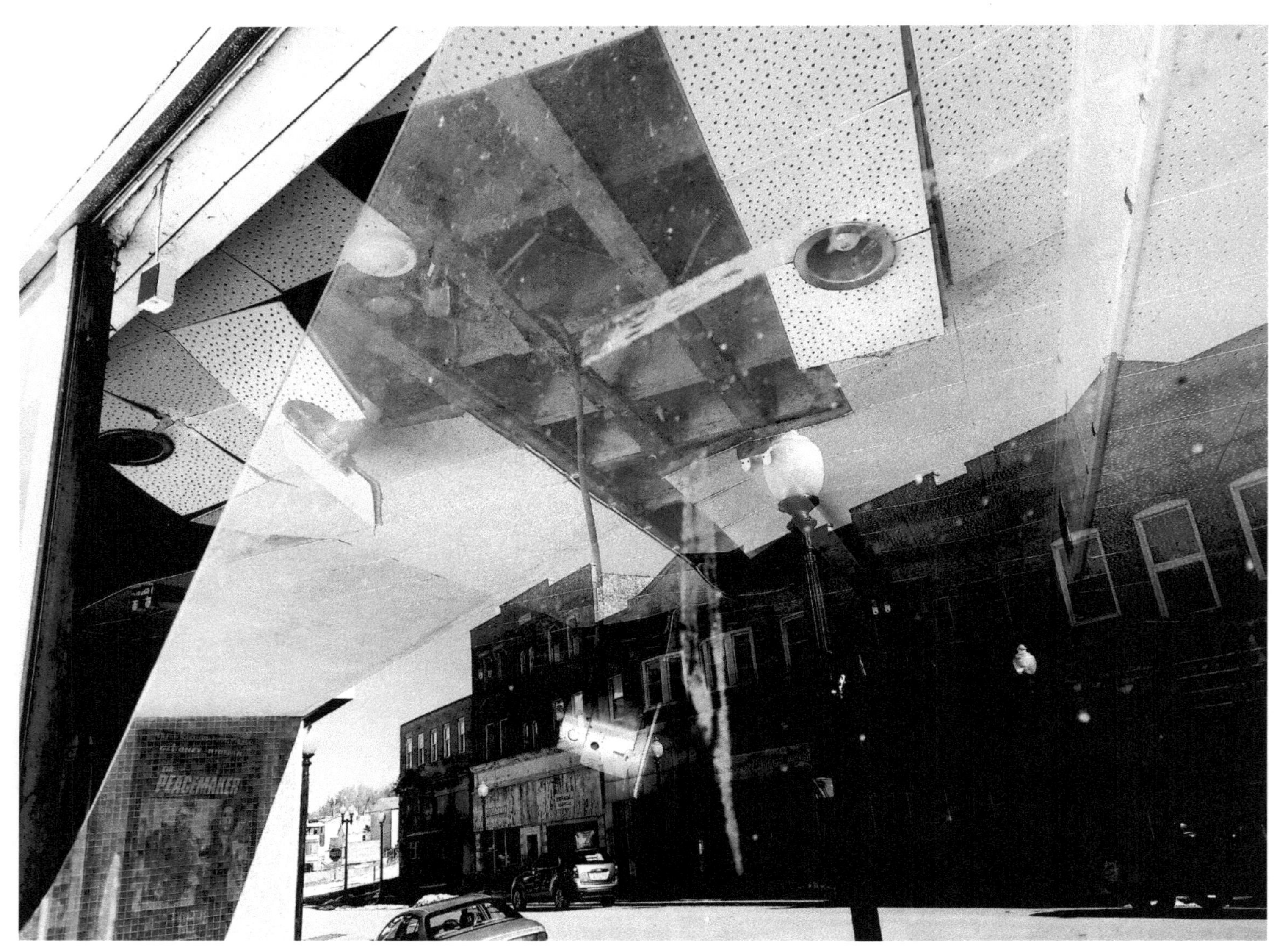

Donora, PA

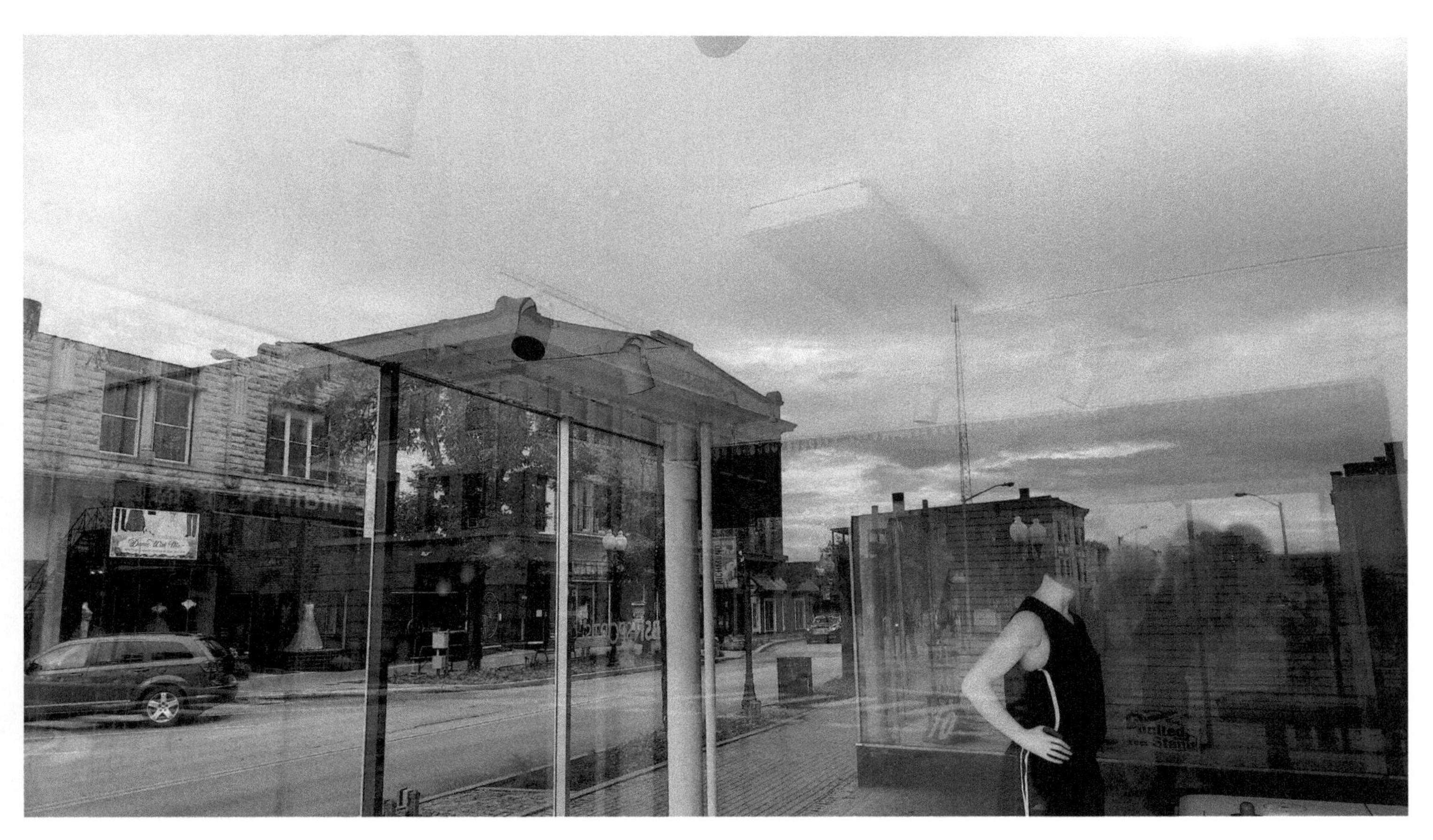

Richmond, IN

29

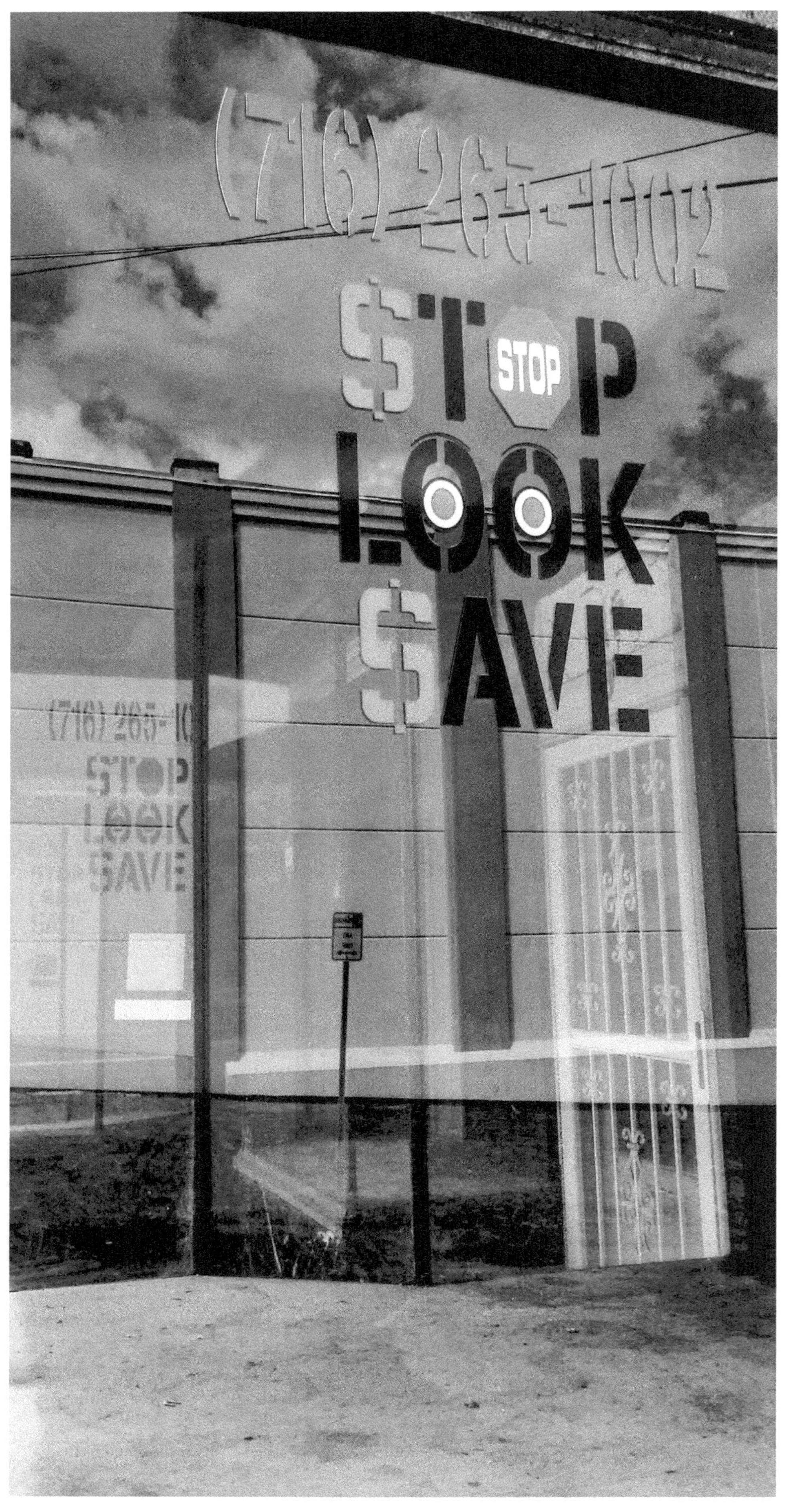

Salamanca, NY

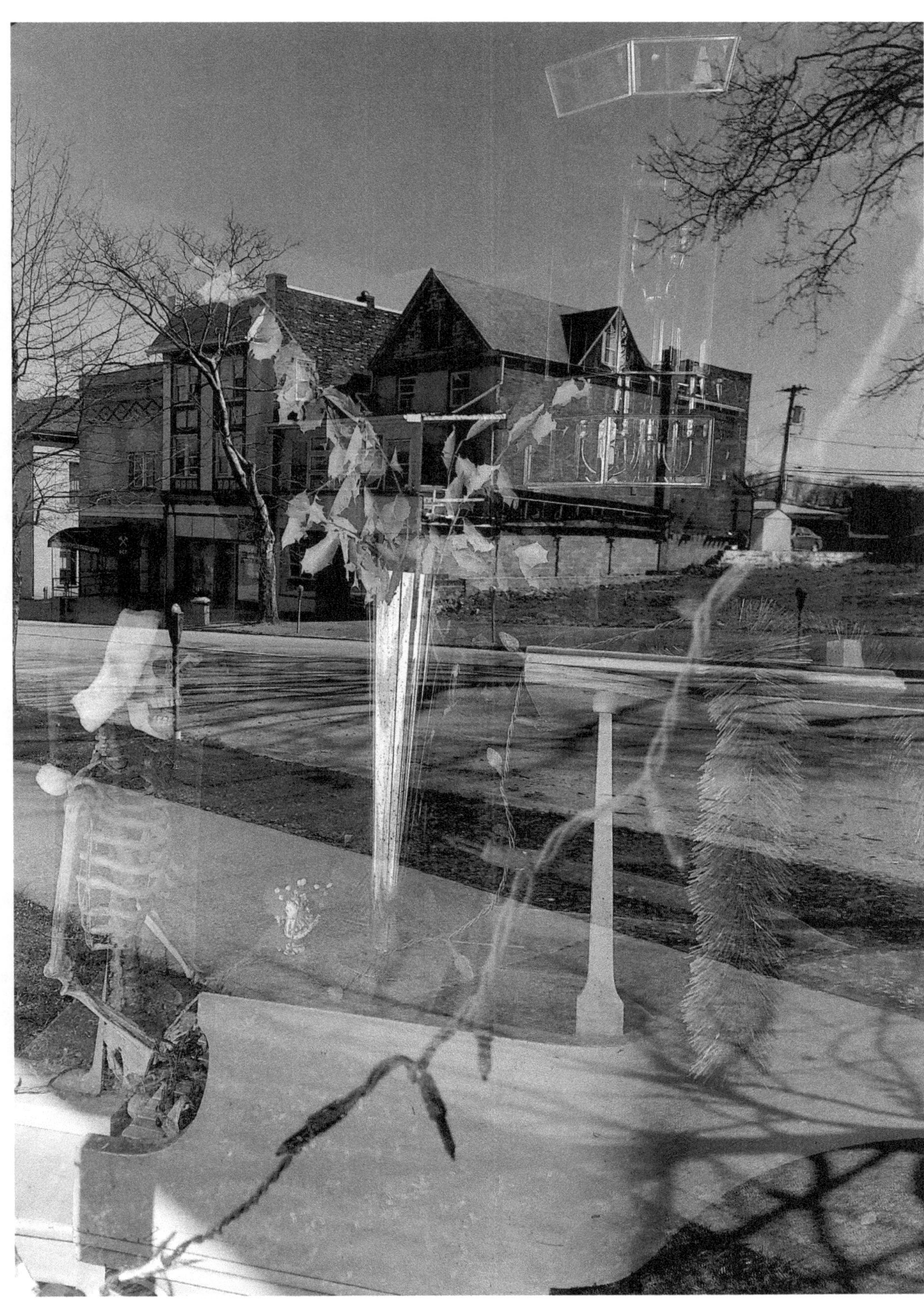

Vandergrift, PA

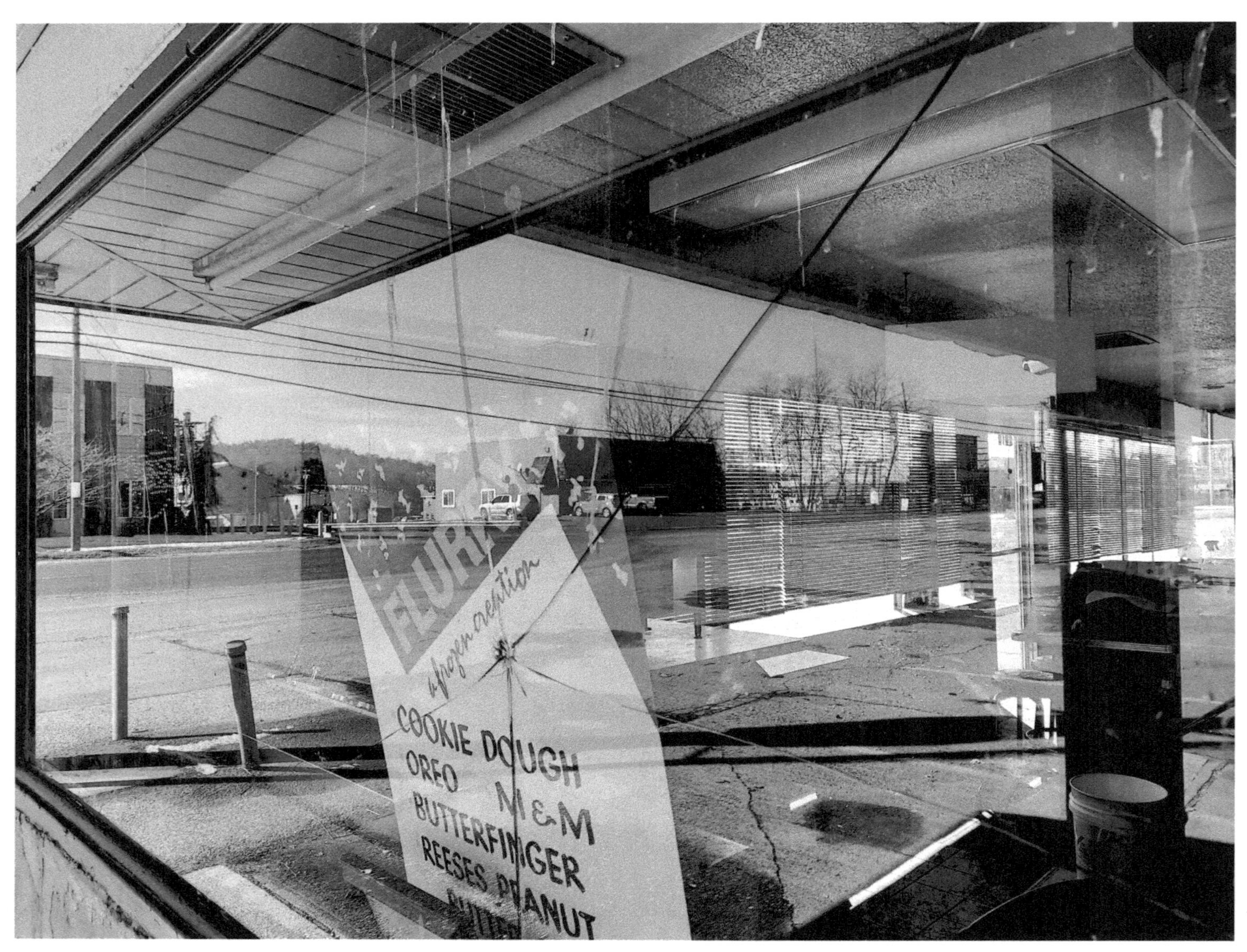

West Elizabeth, PA

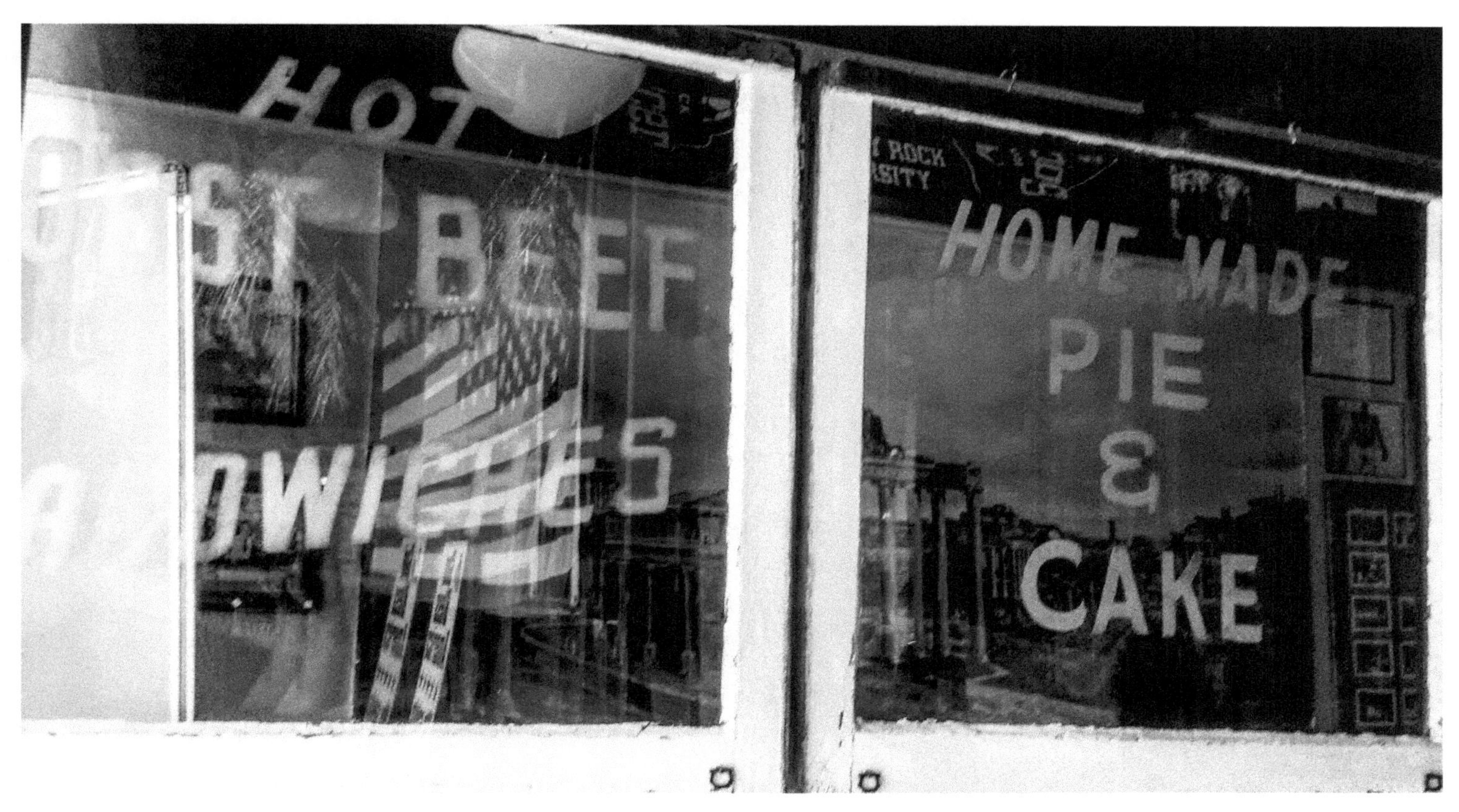

Dubois, PA

Durable Medical Eq
Diabetic Suppl
Continuous Gluco
Medical Suppo

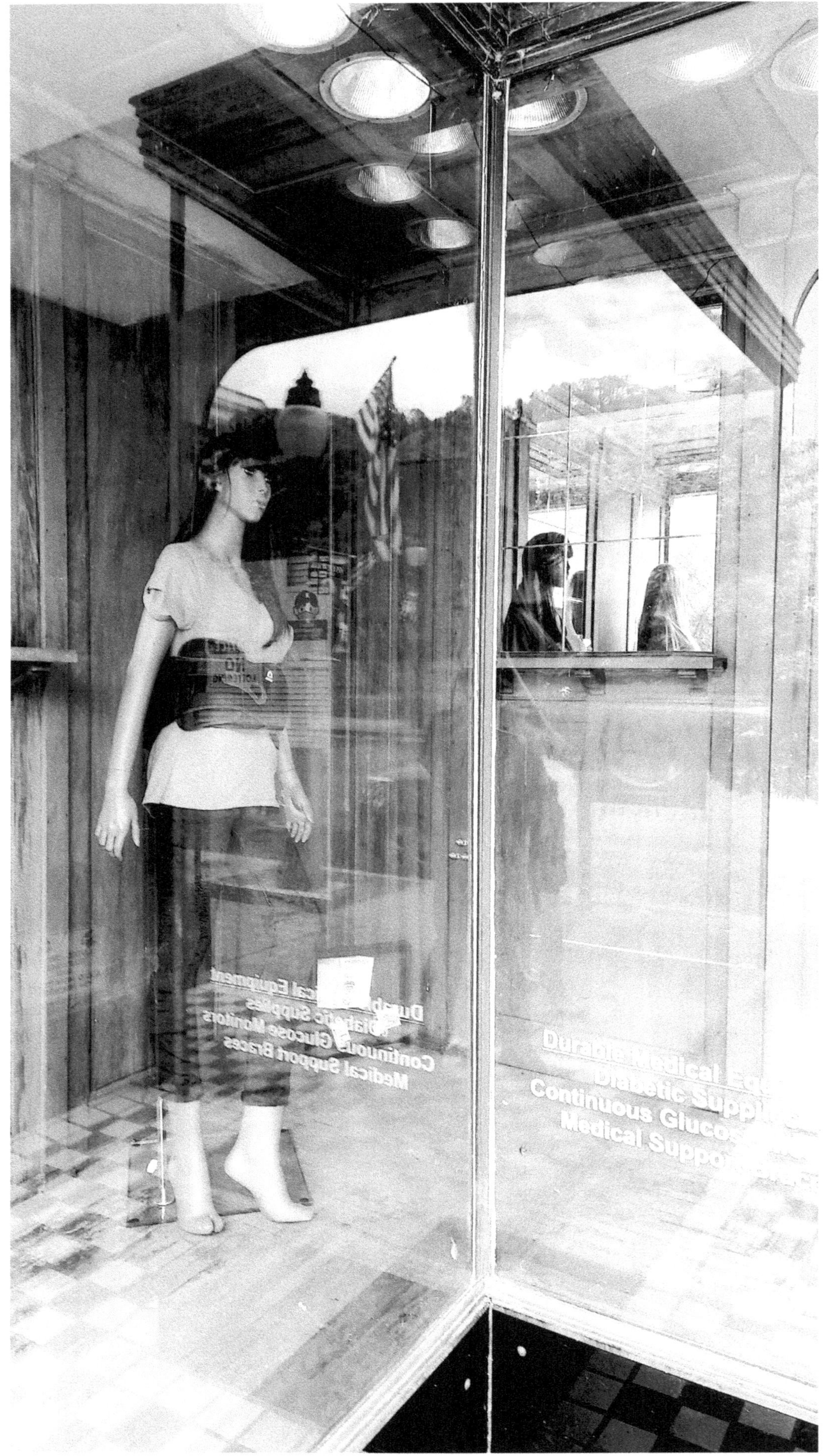

Hinton, WV

WARD'S
TIP-TOP
BREAD
Enriched for Better Nutrition
TIP-TOP
ENRICHED
WARD BAKING COMPANY
Enriched for Better Nutrition

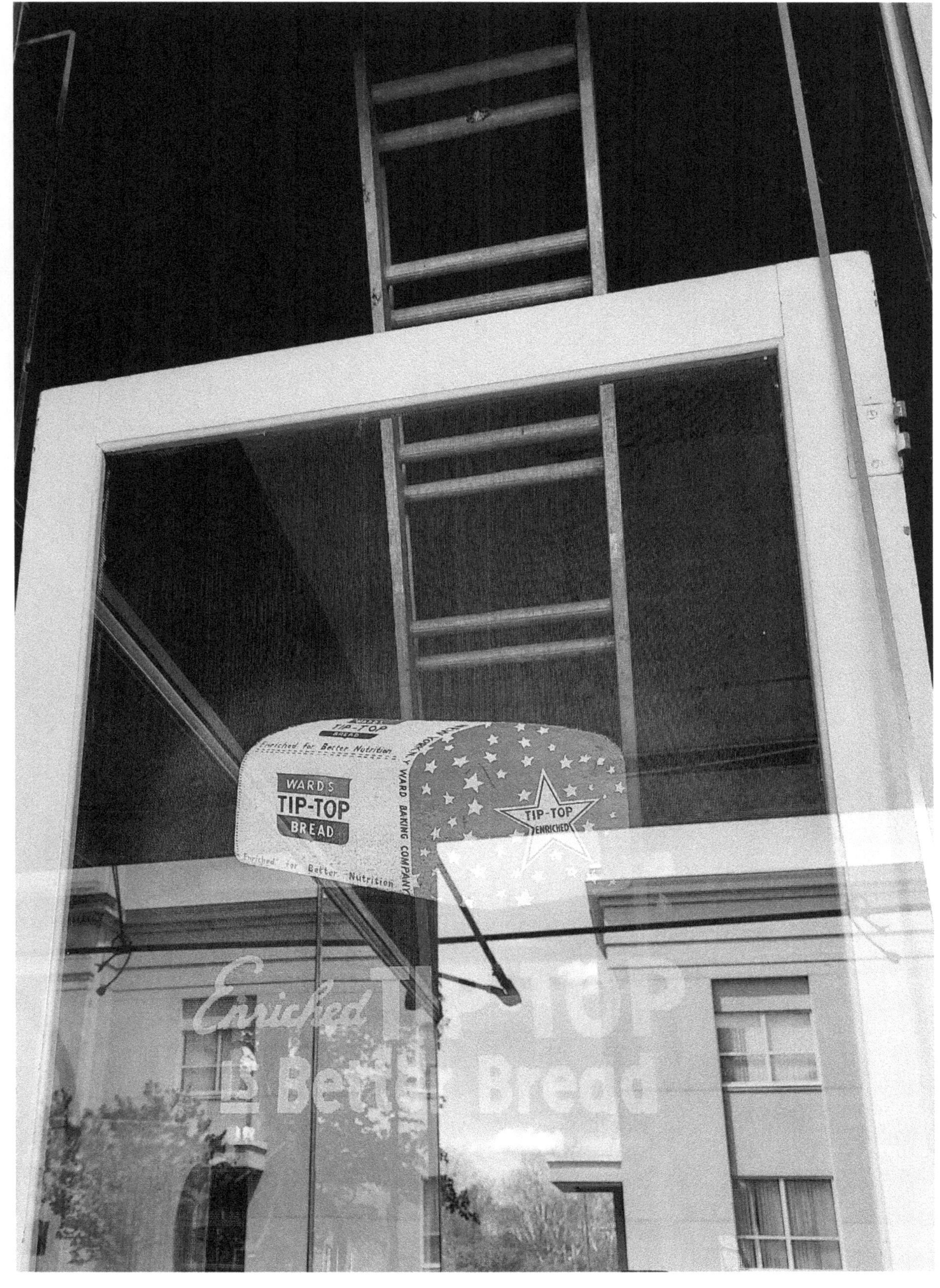

Kinsman, OH

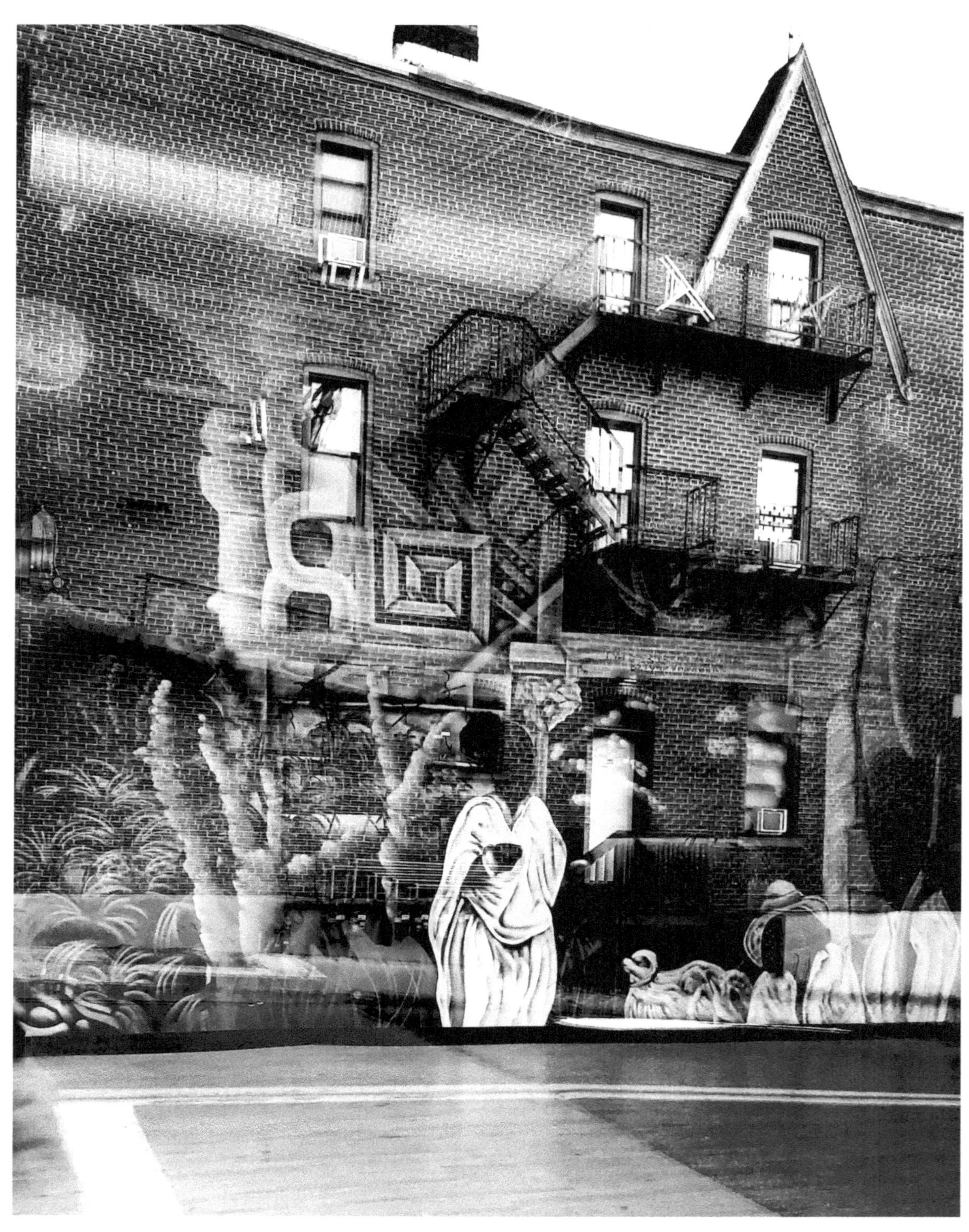

Garfield, PA

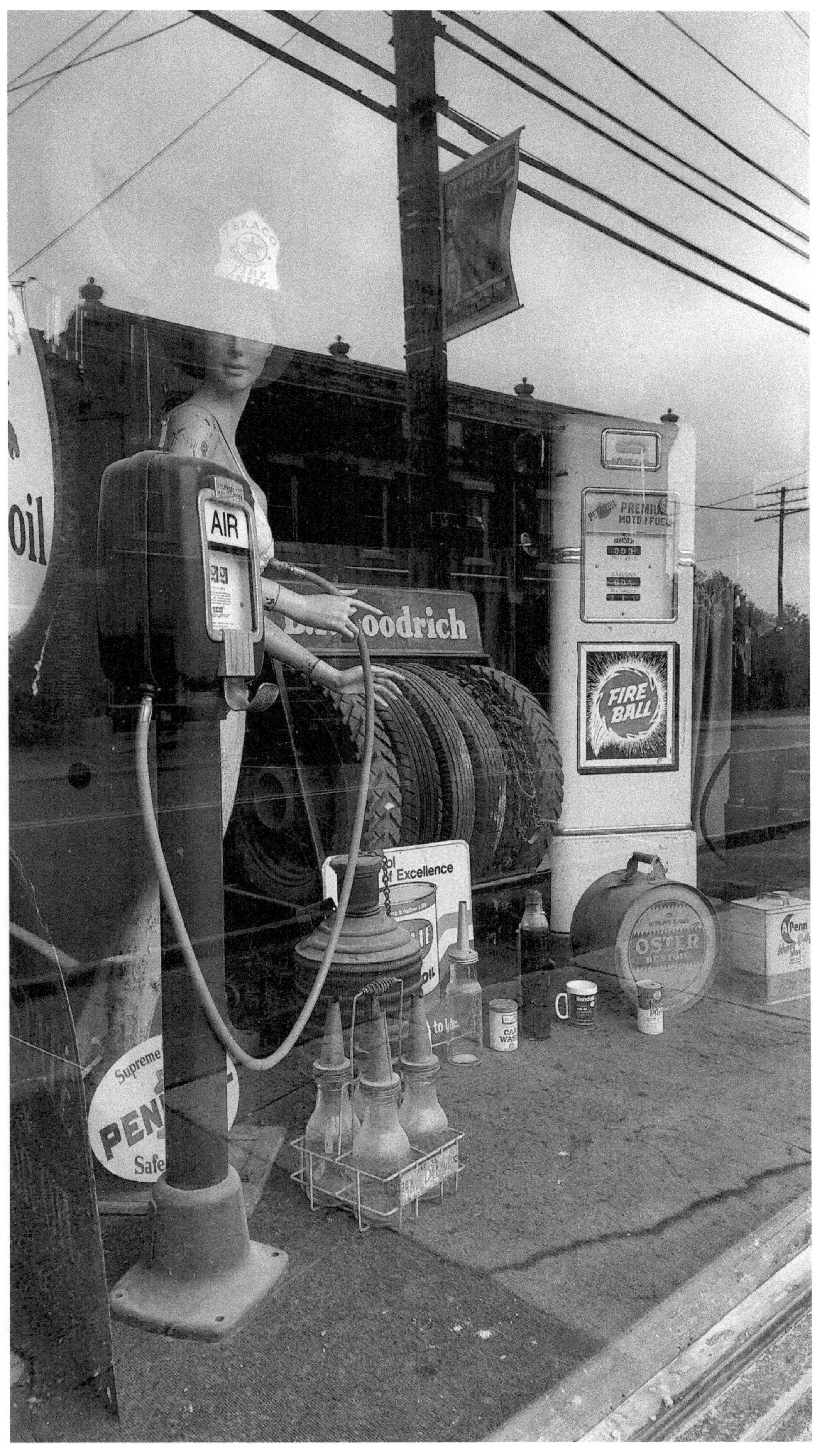

Mount Jewitt, PA

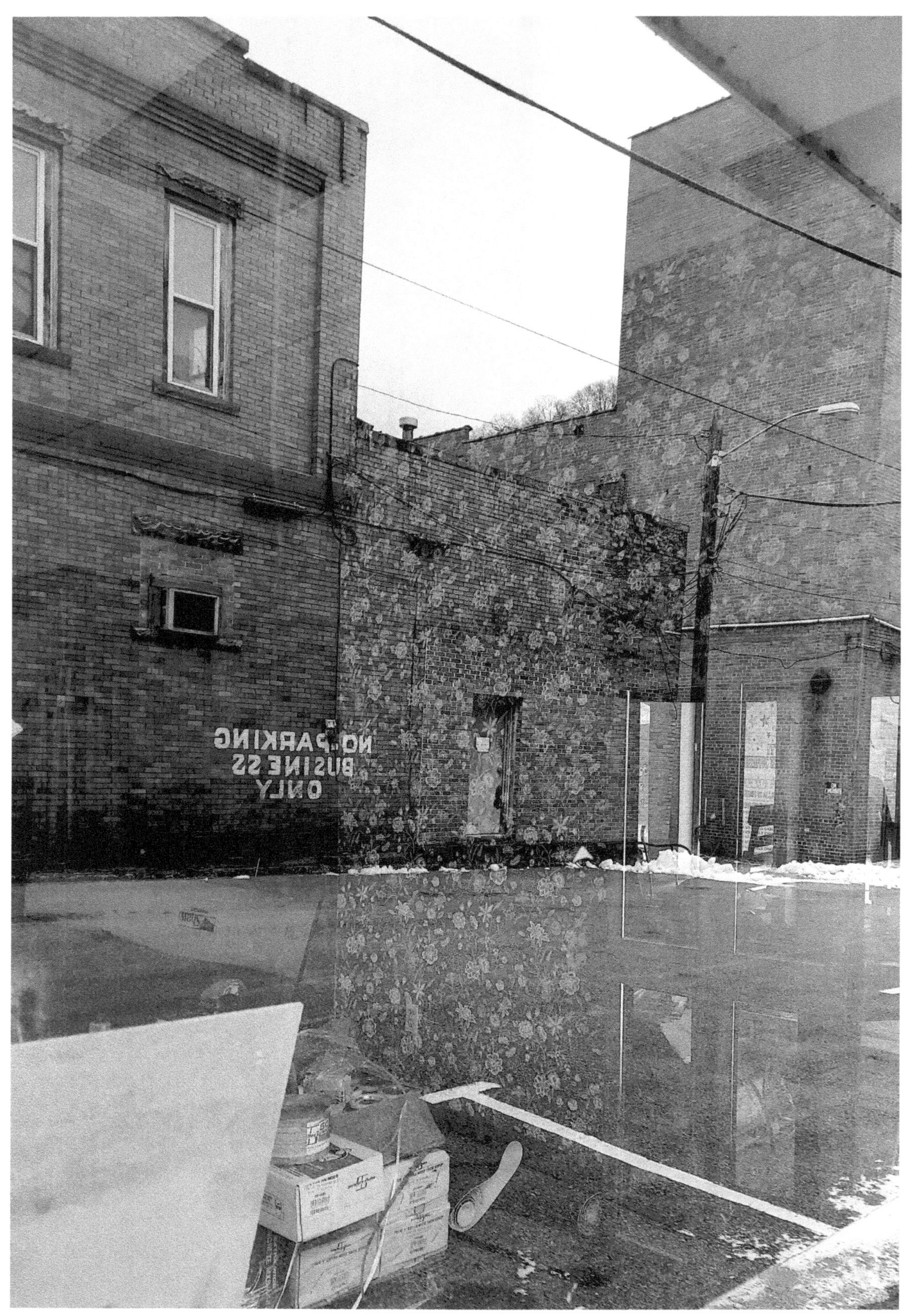

Logan, WV

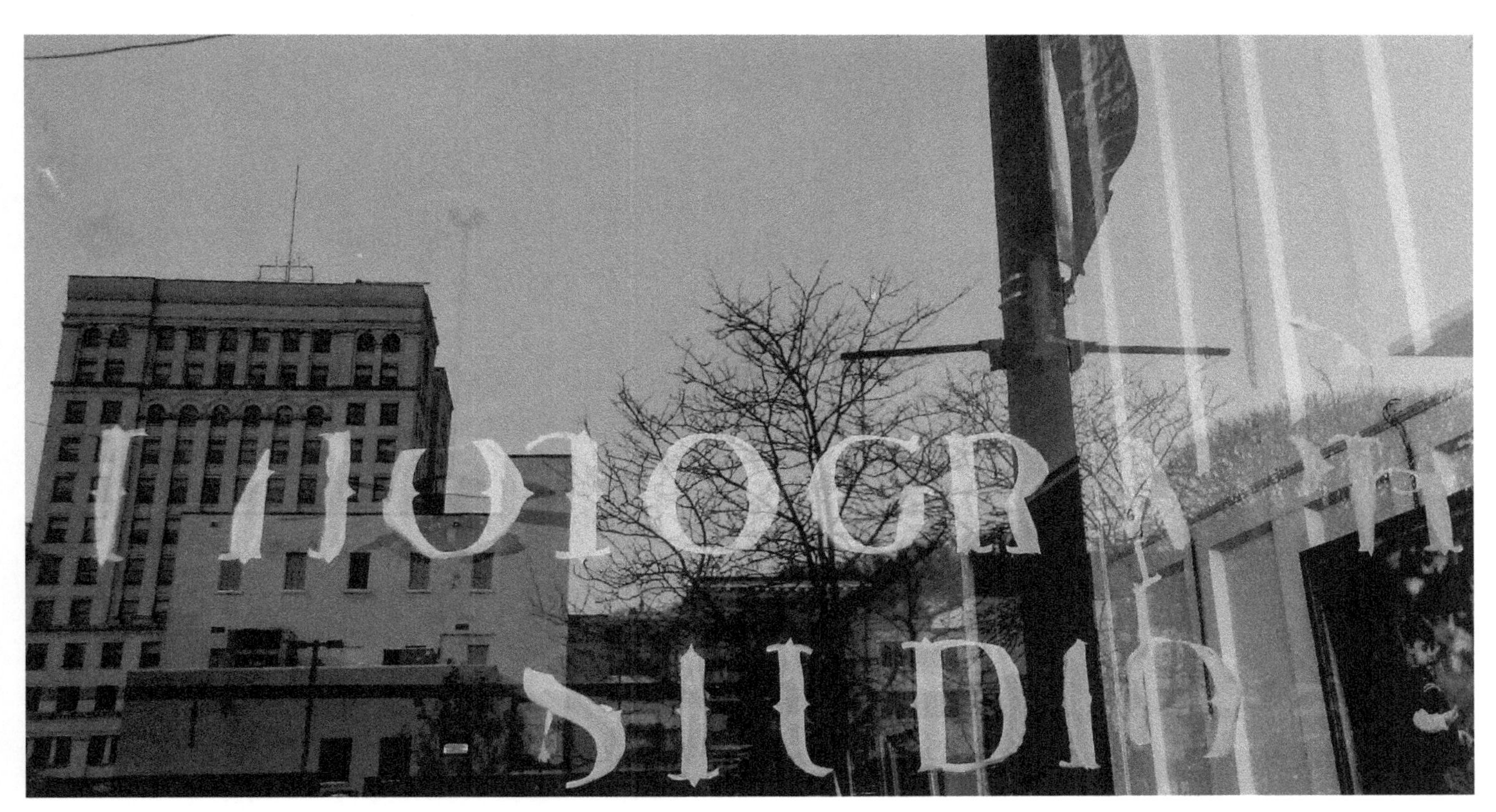

Wheeling, WV

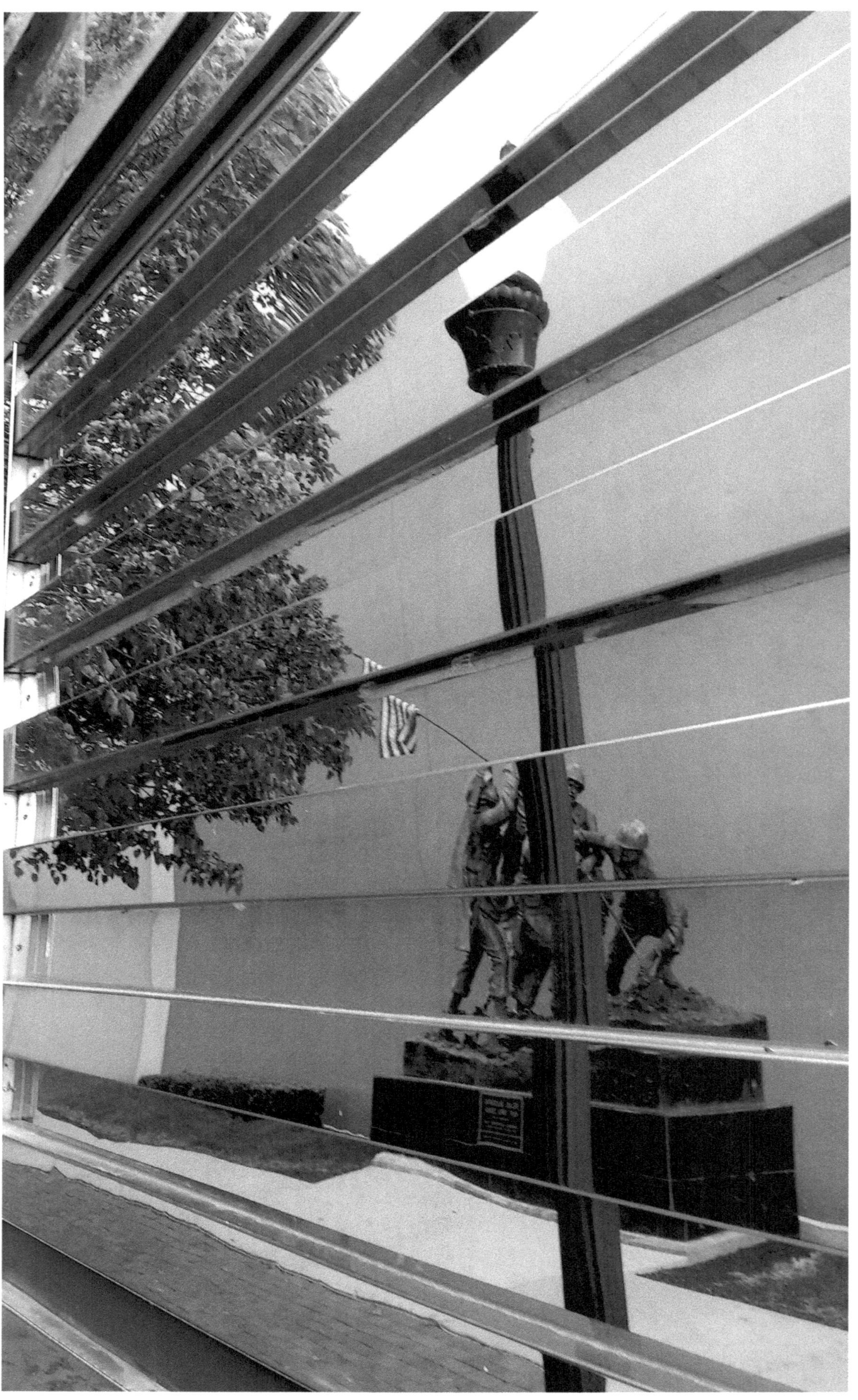

Sharon, PA

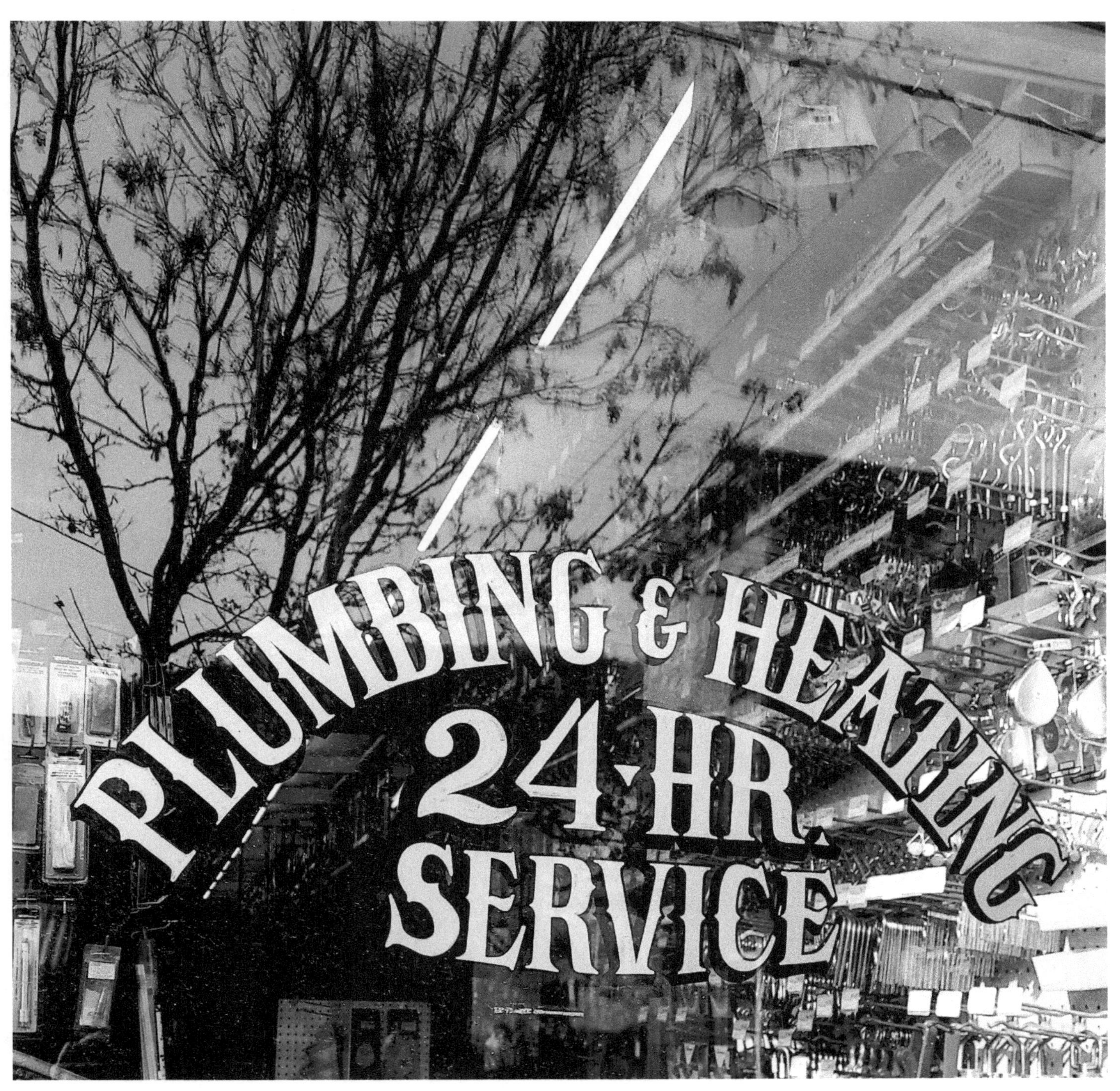

Hancock, NY

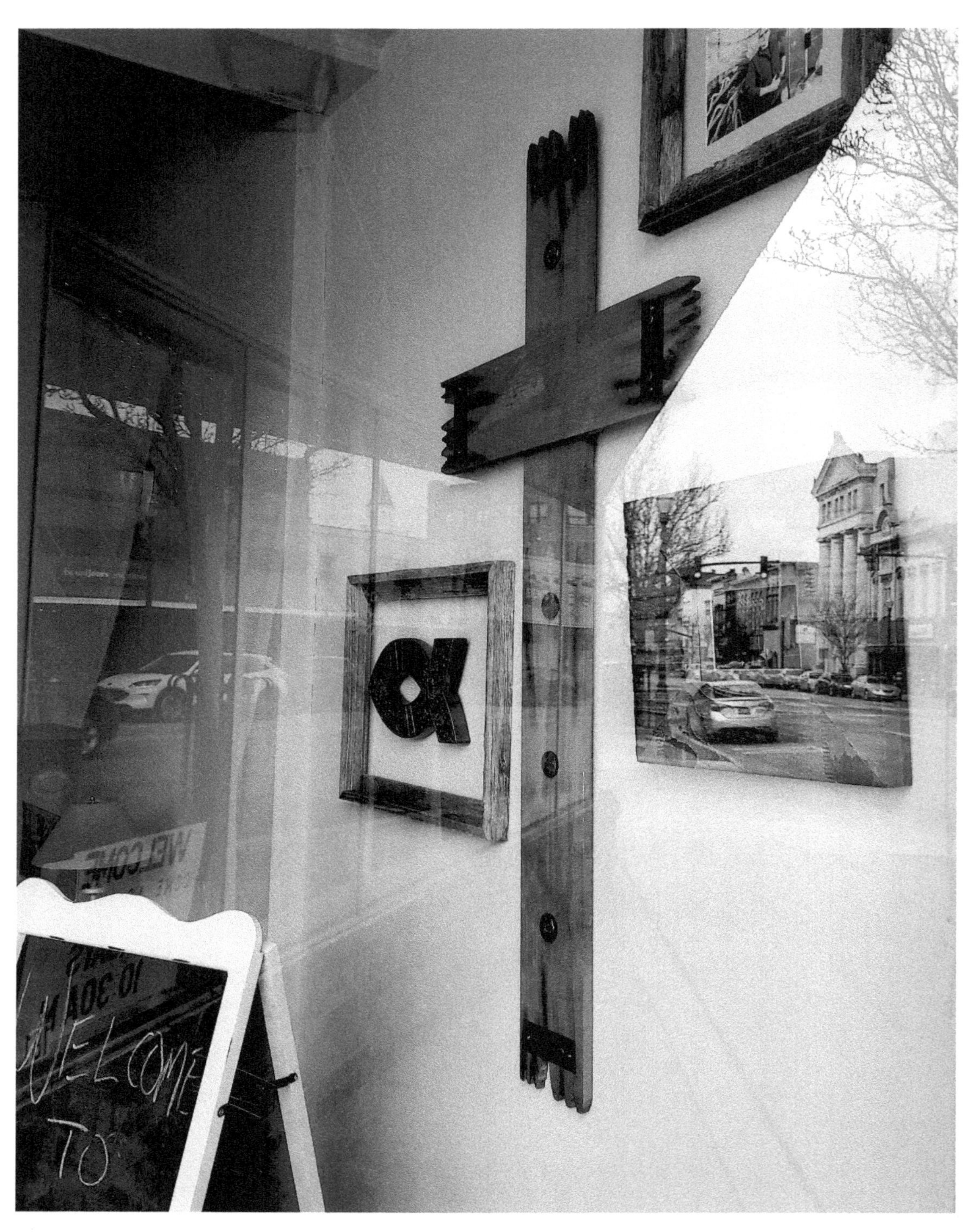

Bowling Green, OH

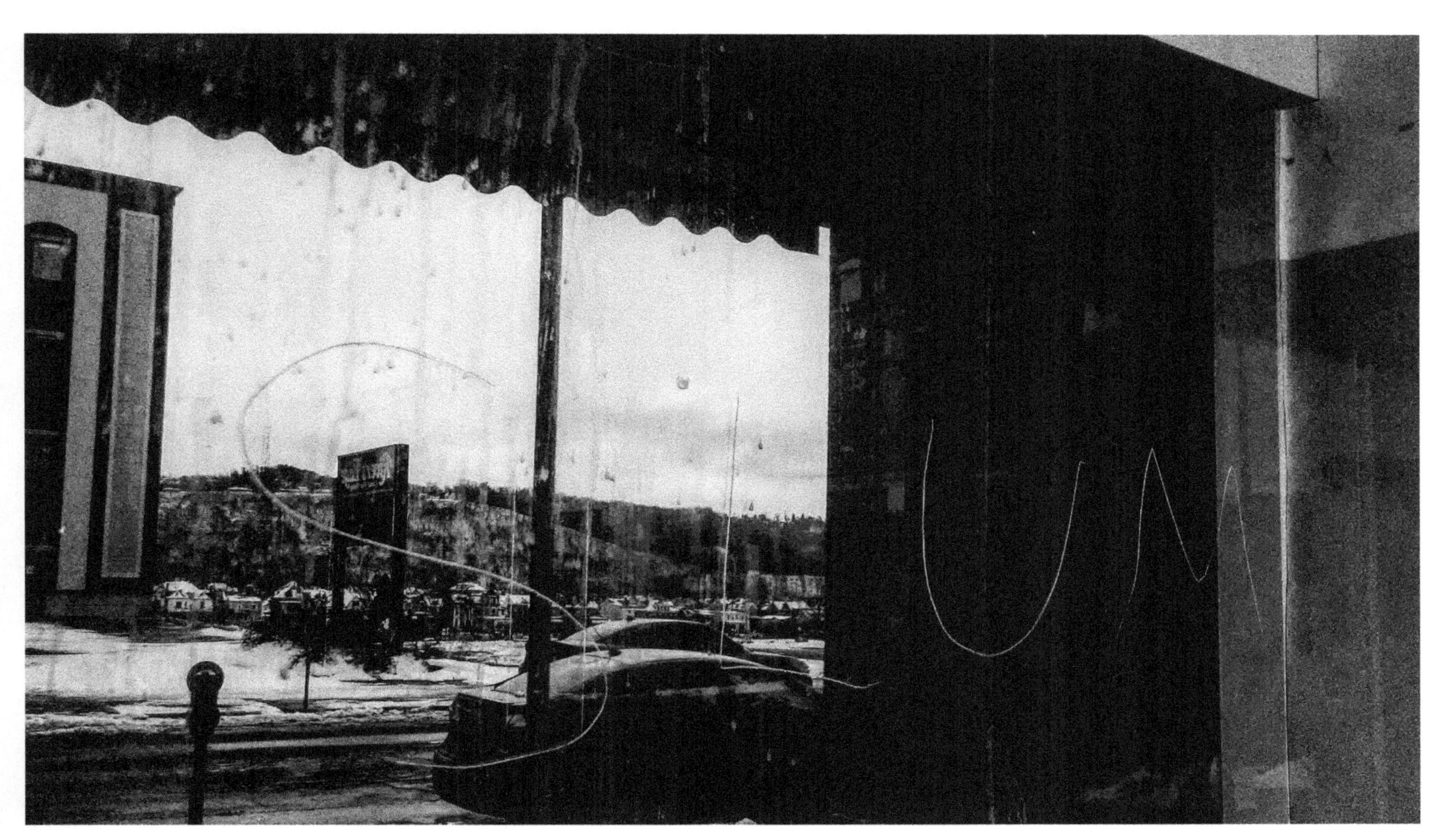

Wheeling, WV

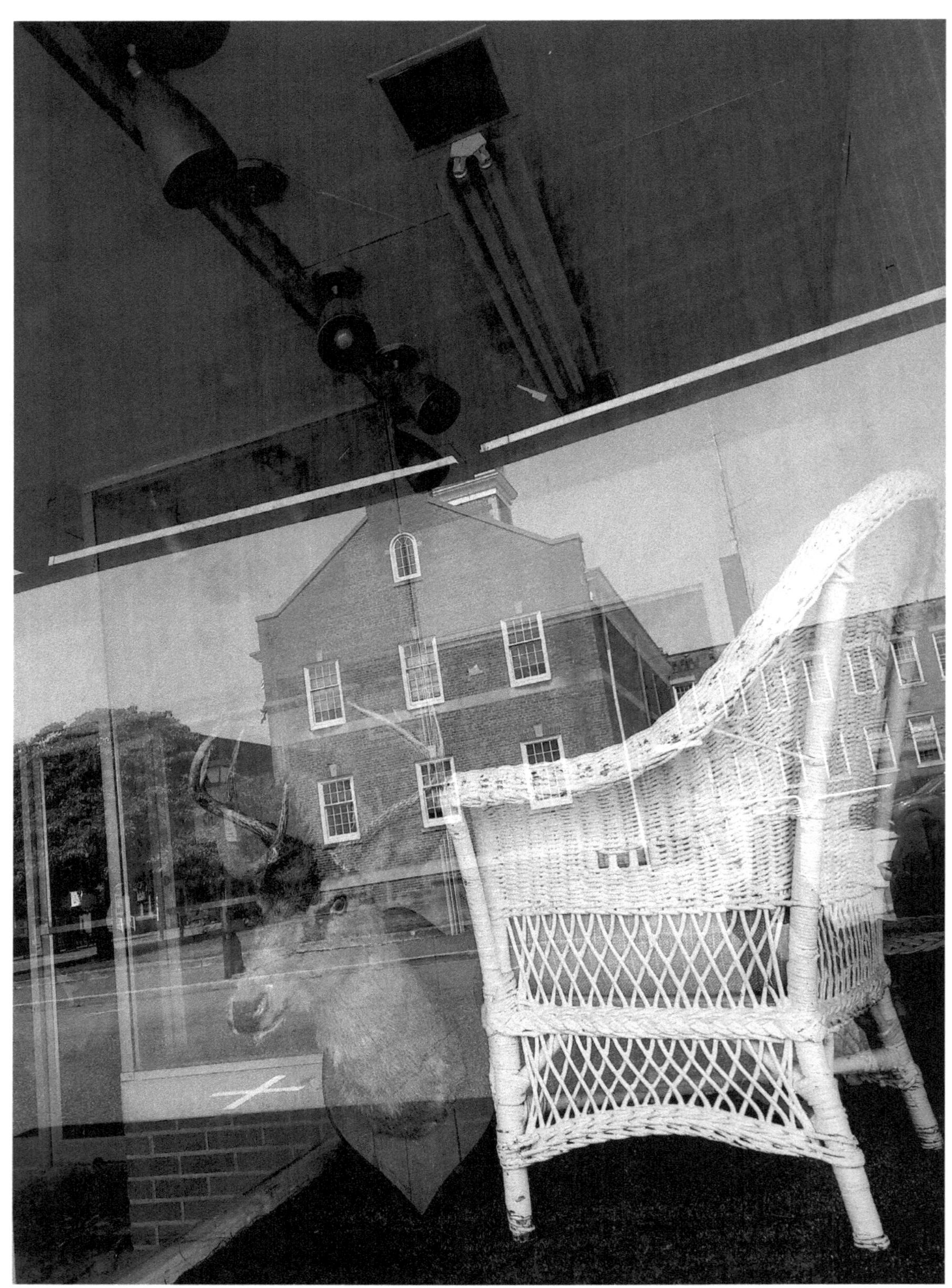

Wellsburg, WV

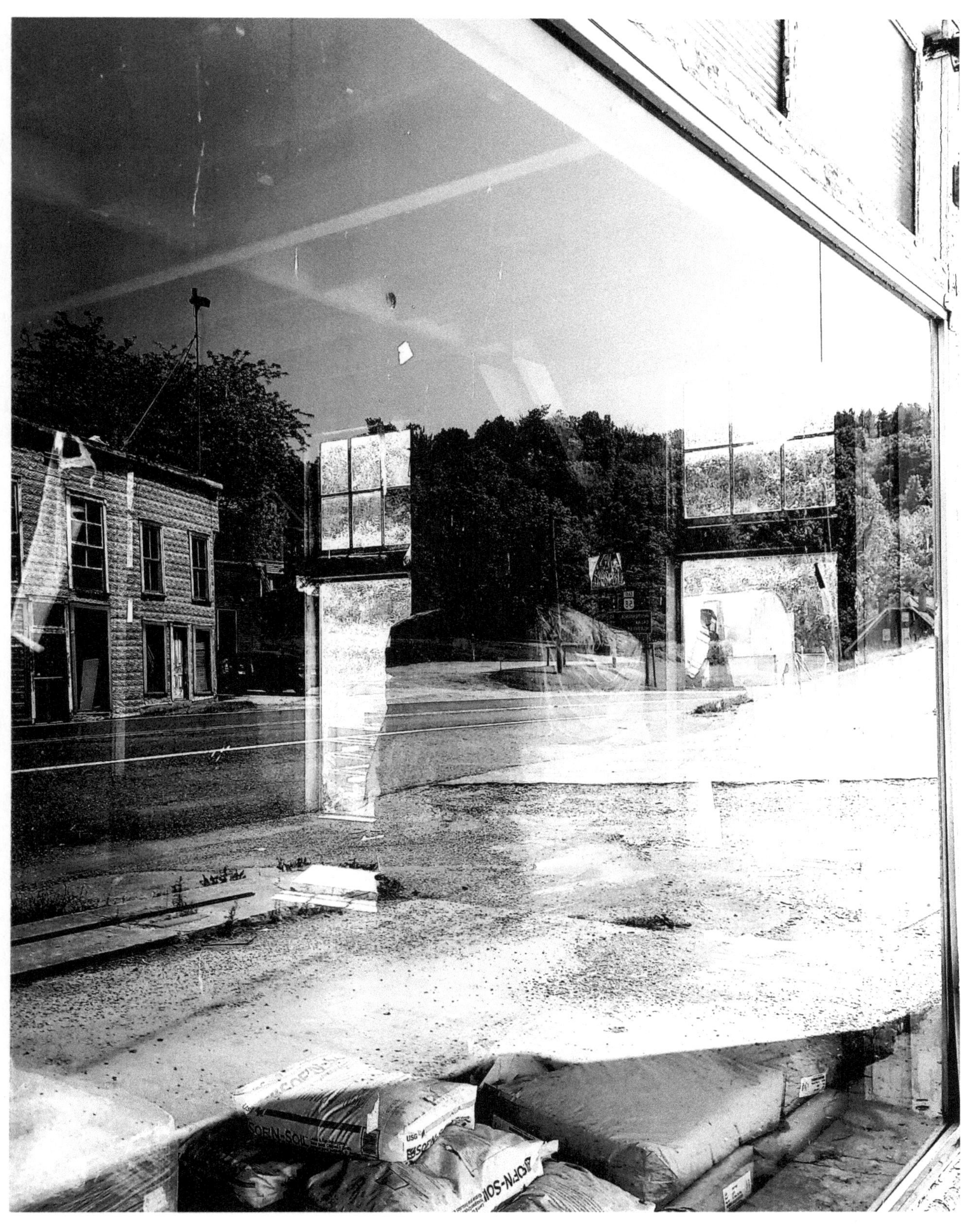

Mouth of Wilson, VA

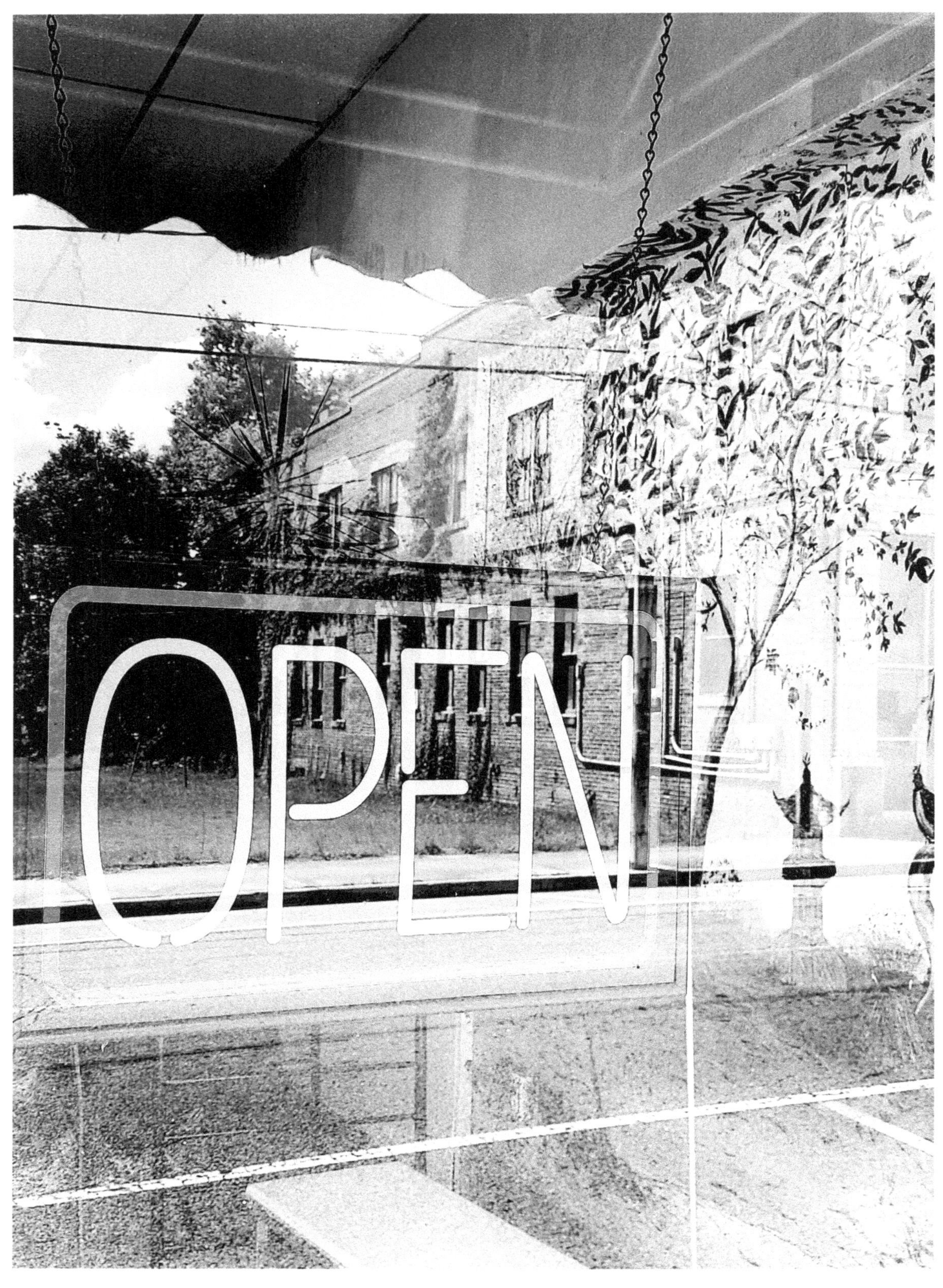

St Matthews, SC

46

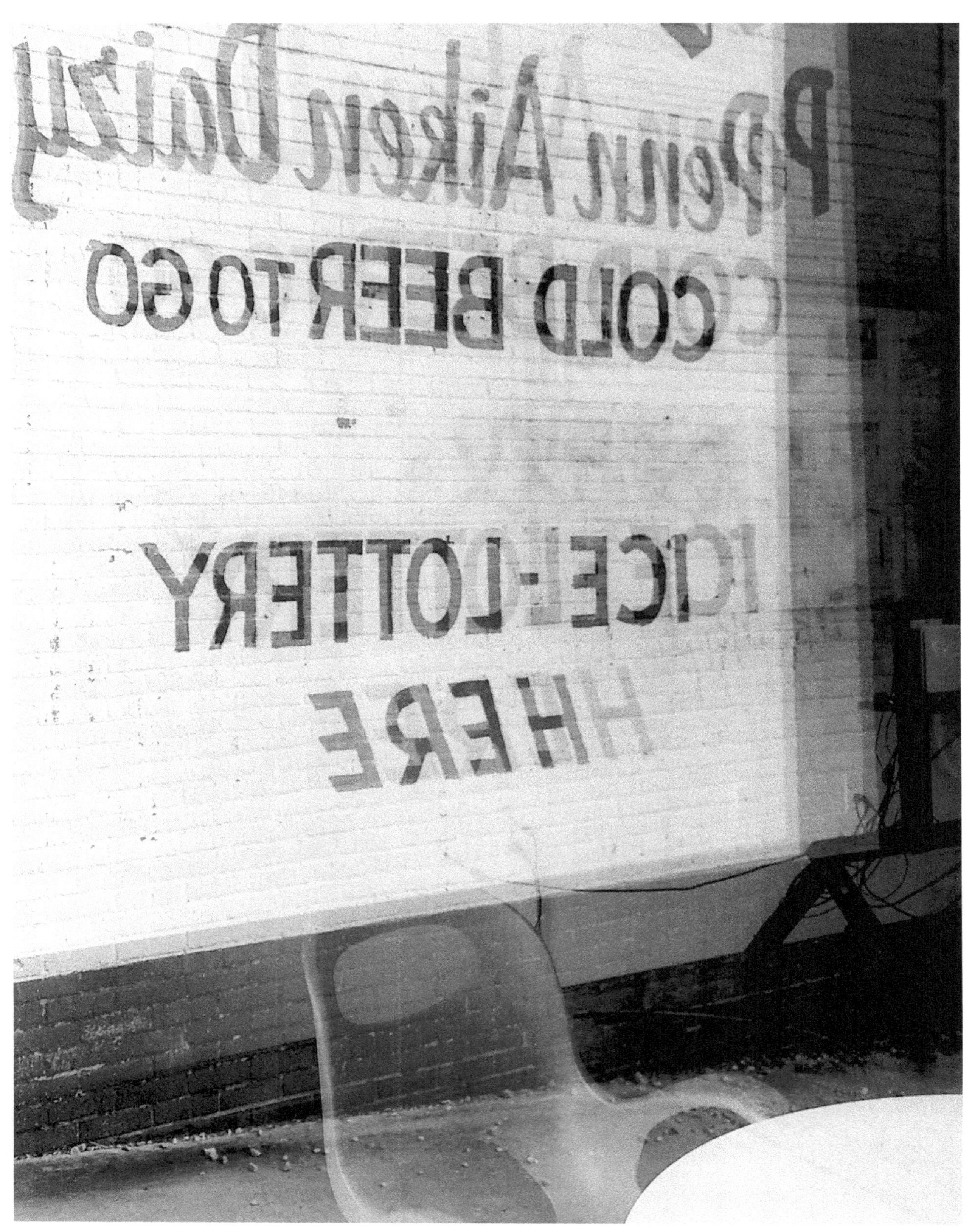

Garfield, PA

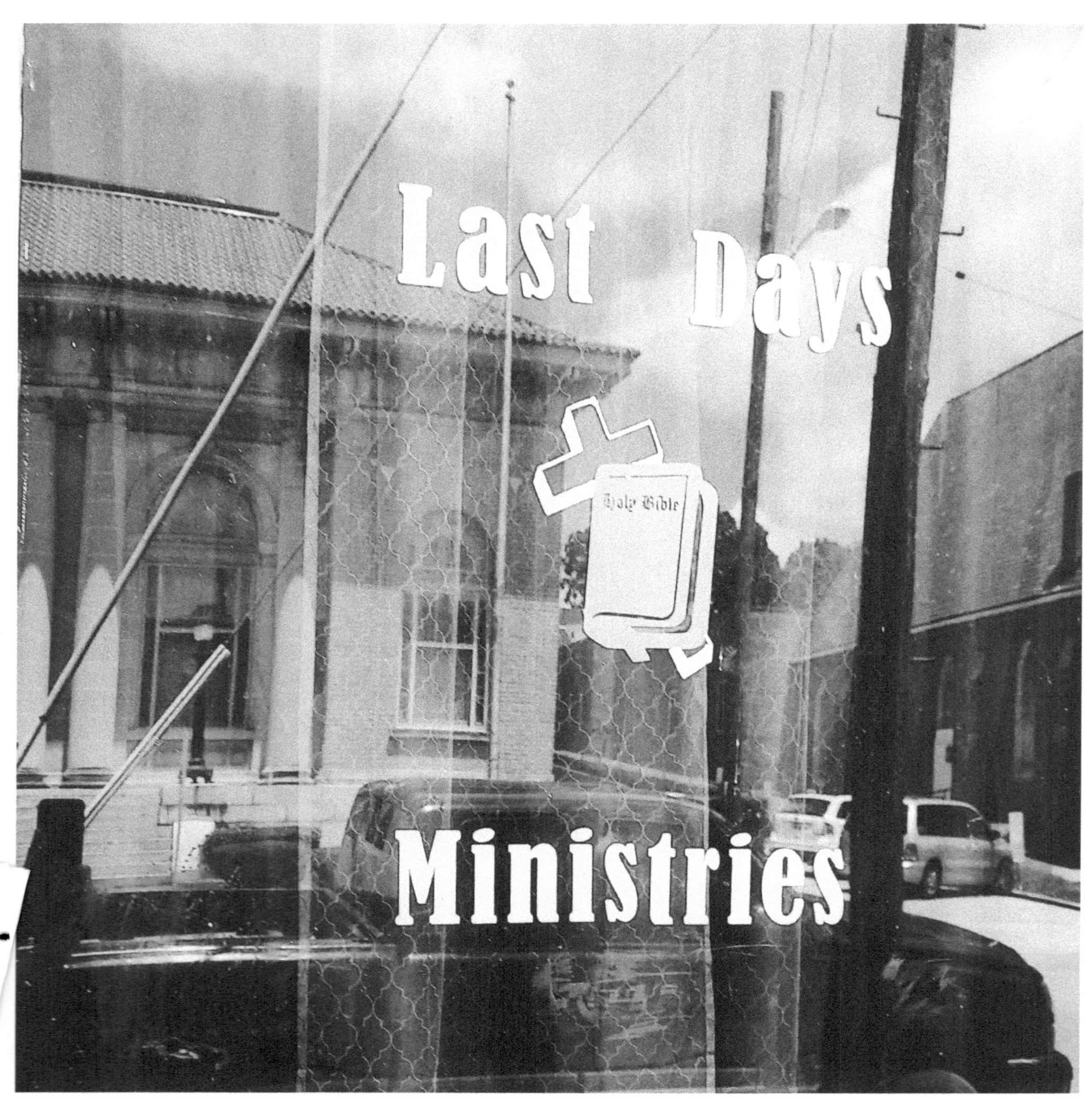

Owingsville, KY

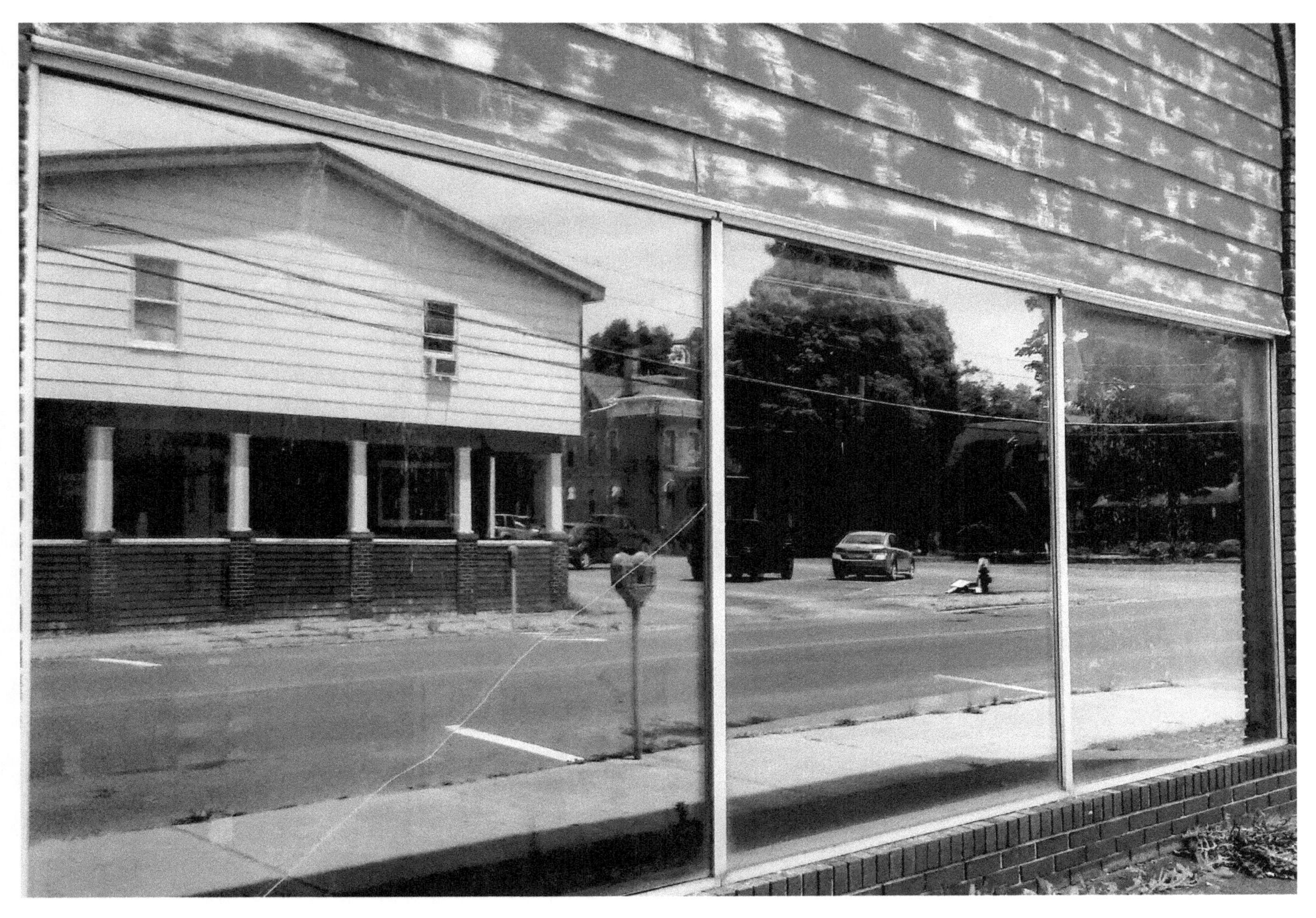

Punxsawtawny, PA

49

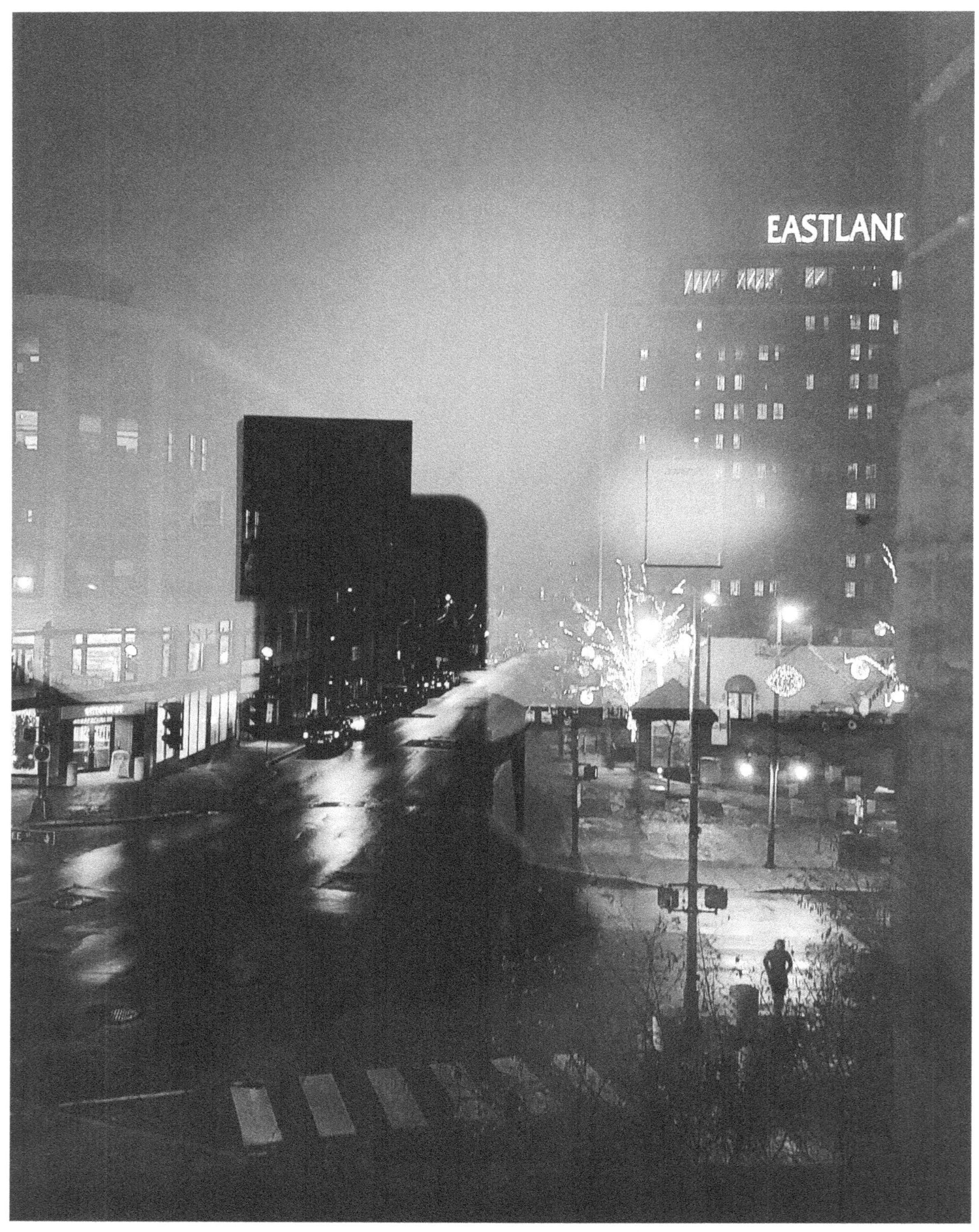

Portland, ME

Jason Baldinger is a poet and photographer
from Pittsburgh, PA. He's penned fifteen
books of poetry the newest of which include:
*A History of Backroads Misplaced: Selected
Poems 2010-2020* (Kung Fu Treachery),
and *This Still Life* (Kung Fu Treachery)
with James Benger. Two ekphrastic
collaborations (with the poets Rebecca
Schumejda and Robert Dean) are forthcoming.

His work has appeared across a wide variety of
online sites and print journals. You can hear
him from various books on Bandcamp and on
lps by The Gotobeds and Theremonster. This is
his first photography collection.

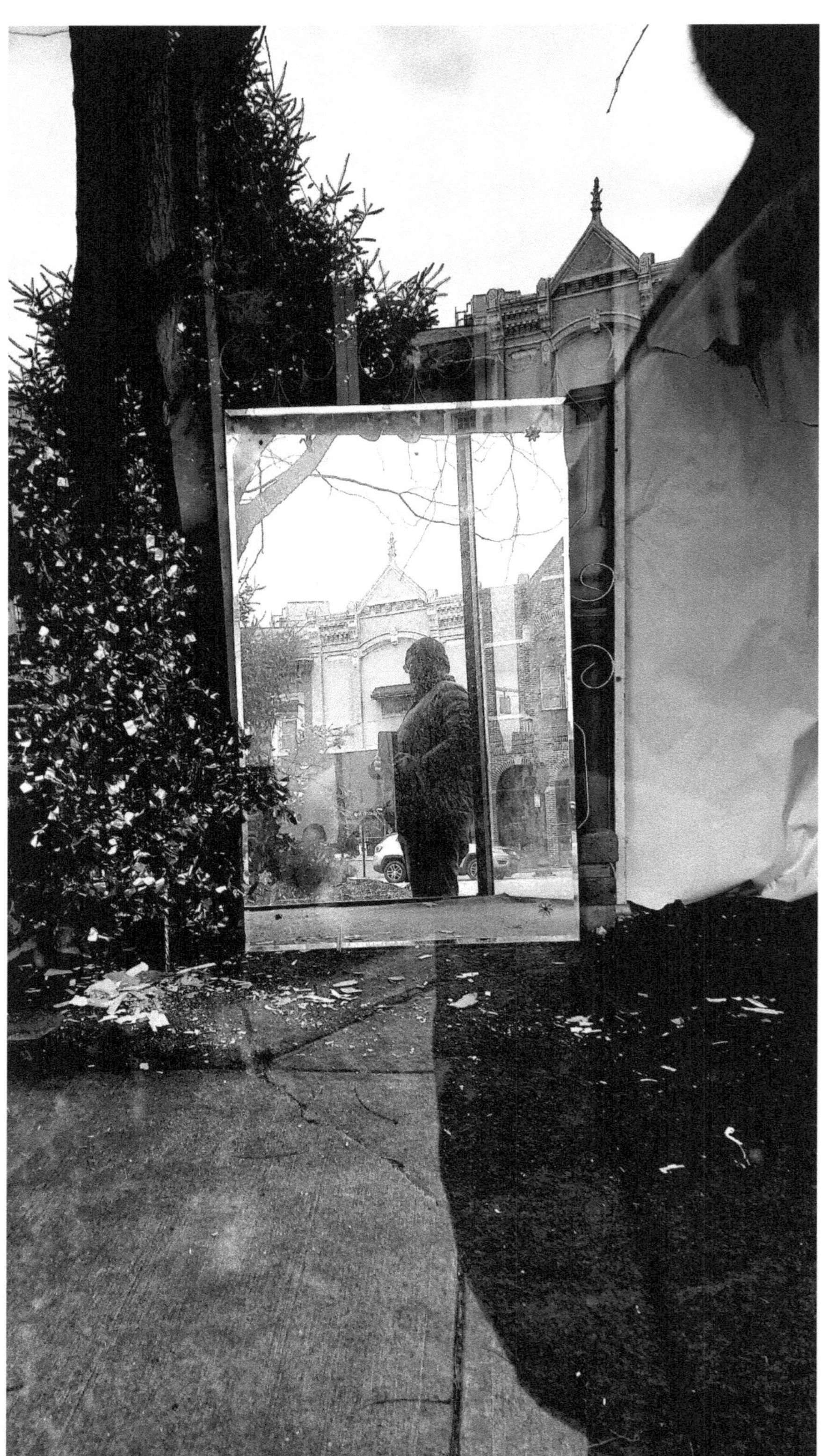

This project was made possible, in part, by generous support from the Osage Arts Community.

Osage Arts Community provides temporary time, space and support for the creation of new artistic works in a retreat format, serving creative people of all kinds — visual artists, composers, poets, fiction and nonfiction writers. Located on a 152-acre farm in an isolated rural mountainside setting in Central Missouri and bordered by ¾ of a mile of the Gasconade River, OAC provides residencies to those working alone, as well as welcoming collaborative teams, offering living space and workspace in a country environment to emerging and mid-career artists. For more information, visit us at www.osageac.org

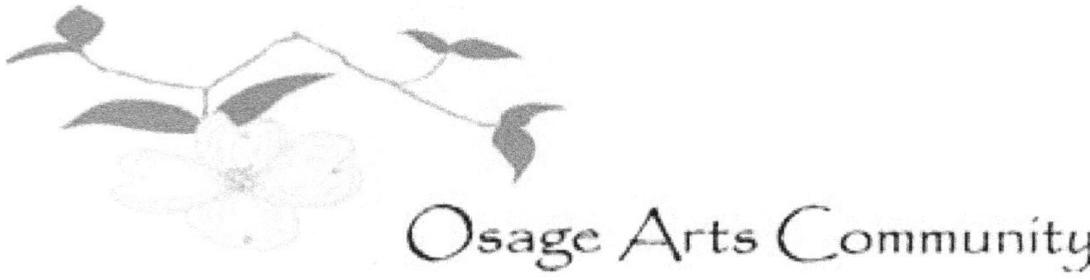